Ana's Wisdom
Leadership Recipes

Ángeles Martínez Valenciano

Ana's Wisdom – Leadership Recipes
All rights reserved.
© 2021, Ángeles Martínez Valenciano
Cover Picture: © Ana María Sánchez Quiroz
Author's Picture: © Luis Vazquez Photography
Pukiyari Publishers

First Published as:
La Sabiduría de Ana – Recetas de Liderazgo
© 2020, Ángeles Martínez Valenciano
ISBN-13: 978-1-63065-132-9

Publisher's note: This book was published in 2020. As of 2023 Ms. Valenciano left NDC to become CEO of TXDC.

The total or partial reproduction of this book is prohibited. This book cannot be totally or partially reproduced, transmitted, copied or stored using any means or ways including graphic, electronics or mechanic without the consent and written authorization of the author, except in the case of small quotes used in articles and written comments about the book.

ISBN-13: 978-1-63065-143-5

PUKIYARI PUBLISHERS
www.pukiyari.com

To my sons, Tony, Diego, and Mario,

the greatest loves of my life.

Table of Contents

Foreword 13
My Favorite Ingredient Is Love 16
Dreams Gone in Smoke 21
A Magical Town 25
A Family With Values 31
Ahead of Their Time 37
Always Do Good. In Every Instance, for Everybody 43
Painful Transitions 47
Cultural Shock in Texas 53
An Immigrant's Experience 65
Sharing Recipes, Connecting Hearts 75
Climbing the Corporate Ladder While Starting a Family ... 81
Dennis Kennedy, The Unexpected Ingredient 89
To Know Ourselves Intimately, We Must Figure Out Our Weak Spots 97
The Audacity of Starting From Scratch 101
Cancer and Good-Bye 115
Searching for a New Balance 123
How to Be a Successful Leader 131
Ingredients of Success For Immigrant Women 139
The Art of Transforming Problems Into Solutions 145
The Circle of Influence 155
My Second Mom 165
Diversity-Equity-Inclusion 171
The Unsung Heroes 185

I close my eyes and fall into a wellspring of happiness. I'm joyfully walking in San Luis Potosí. Its history-filled streets take me through adventurous paths that discover before my eyes the most beautiful town in México. I can see myself as I was back then, dark, tall, thin. My long, straight hair, as lustrous and slick as polished black onyx, tamed for the weekday in thick braids. My playful arms moving on both sides of my body, touching my hips as they go back and forth. My eyes, two blackened almonds, frolic like butterflies that have just left their cocoon behind and are enraptured by everything they see. I breathe in the wonderful aroma of hot bread made in an old firewood oven. I move freely, observing my people, the color of their clothes announcing their arrival from afar. Land of the Náhuatl, Huasteco, Pame and Otomí, which to this day has their cultural flavors imprinted everywhere. It was the greed of the Spaniards for its gold and silver that brought them to our region. They thought the mines in San Luis Potosí could be as rich as the ones in Potosí, Bolivia. And even though they couldn't achieve their dream, they still blended their Spanish culture with that of those already living here. The cobbled passages take me to different places, especially to wonderful churches run by Jesuits, Augustinians, and Franciscans, standing formidable throughout my route, reminding me of my Catholic roots.

My mother always told me I should never forget where I come from. Now, that I'm so far away in distance and time, I remember more than ever.

Wearing a regional dress. San Luis Potosí, age thirteen.

Foreword

By Dennis Kennedy
Former Chairman and Founder of the NDC

Eighteen years ago, I was at the JP Morgan Chase Texas headquarters in San Antonio, trying to make the case for what was then the Texas Diversity Council. I didn't get the financial support I came looking for but got away with something even more valuable: Ángeles Martínez Valenciano. She was starting a new job at a high level in that corporate giant and, somehow, I had the audacity to ask her to run away with me and help me build my vision. Against all odds, she did it.

When I met Ángeles I was immediately taken aback in amazement by what I saw inside her. I knew I had found my other half, and I was not mistaken. When you start an initiative from scratch, such as the Texas Diversity Council at first, and later the National Diversity Council, the leaders wear multiple hats. She has worn each hat in style without ever missing a beat. She is an overcomer with no quit in her DNA.

It's been such a privilege to watch her evolve and grow into the wonderful leader she's today. Ángeles makes a difference wherever she goes while role-modeling for others all the characteristics of a servant leader: listening, empathy, awareness, stewardship, building a community, growth, serving others, developing talent, mentoring and so much more.

Research shows that the success of an organization is predicated upon its leadership. I am the one who dreams it and she is the one that makes it happen. And as the person that takes my vision and makes it into something real, Ángeles works hard and extremely smart to take my ideas and provide the strategy and direction needed, encouraging everyone with her passion, commitment and determination to keep going until the goals are reached. The National Diversity Council would not be what it is today, growing from a state entity to a national presence, providing direction for well over four-hundred corporate members, without the uniqueness and perseverance that Ángeles brought to the table. From her I've learned to be patient while relentlessly working toward a goal that at times seems so far away.

Selecting Ángeles back when I was first starting and now as our CEO was unequivocally the right decision. There are so many special ingredients she's brought to the National Diversity Council, our staff, the communities, our partners, and myself, that I'd need an entire book to go through them, but I'll mention her execution of strategy, her individual drive, her unwavering commitment, and her vision. She is a passionate leader everybody trusts. Yes, she is the perfect CEO. She has successfully built a national organization that impacts almost all major cities in the United States. Her leadership is profound. She is trusted and admired by our staff. She is an inclusive leader and leads collaboratively. The National Diversity Council has grown each year she has been our CEO. She deserves much of the credit for the growth of the NDC.

Even as we were starting out with pretty much nothing but our strong determination, I could tell Ángeles would take us much further than I could have ever dreamed. When we were putting together our first conference, our entire volunteer staff responsible for organizing the event decided to quit. Ángeles stepped in and almost single-handedly organized a three-day conference which turned out amazing.

It is always a great idea to surround ourselves with people who are different from us, with people who will complement us, with people who will teach us. As an African American male, I have learned so much about the Latino community from Ángeles. She is an immensely proud immigrant who loves her home country of México and has a relentless love for all immigrants in this country. She is not ashamed of her heritage and is extremely comfortable speaking about being an immigrant in a country that is not always very welcoming to immigrants. As a servant leader,

Ángeles brings into the mix her passion for the work, for her culture and for her people. From her I've learn not to fear a society that does not accept you and to always be bold.

Above all, she is committed to championing Diversity, Inclusion and Equity everywhere she goes. Because she has a strong desire to bring positive change to the world, her commitment and her tenacity to be bold and lend her voice to this important cause ultimately impacts many people in this country. She is pushing doors open that have been closed for so long. She is fearless in her efforts. Ángeles is smart, strategic, passionate, caring and has a vision for change. She is not waiting for someone else to lead. She is not a leader who leads from the back. In fact, she is rushing to the front to lead.

As I think of Ángeles and all that she's brought to my life, to the National Diversity Council and to the world, I can't help but wish a world full of people like her. It is my sincere hope that the people reading this book will find a way to make it so.

My Favorite Ingredient Is Love

There's a future woman growing within every girl, a chrysalis from which one day a beautiful butterfly will emerge.

The next pages are meant to take the readers through my story and my struggle, from my humble but incredibly happy beginnings as a little girl, to the teenager searching for answers and goals, to the women that I evolved into when I found myself, my peace, and my place in this world.

This is my story.

This is the story of so many women that, like me, came to the United States looking for that special place that would help them become all that they should be emotionally, physically, spiritually, and professionally.

I worked very hard to become successful. But to reach this point in my life it was not something I achieved on my own, I was fortunate so many incredible individuals helped and supported me through rough times, always providing deep wisdom and shining their special light to guide me, always encouraging me not to give up or quit.

The first angel in my life was my own mother, Ana María Sánchez Quiroz. As a young child, she guided and taught me so much. Later, she continued to pass on even more of her knowledge to me as I became a young woman. Her legacy is my legacy. Her wisdom is what I share in this book.

When I first started writing this book, the worldwide COVID-19 pandemic had just begun. It was March of 2020, and the world was drastically changed forever. Then came the murder of George Floyd. It was May. The world watched in horror as a police officer knelt for eight minutes and forty-six seconds on the neck of an African American man, suspected of passing a fake twenty-dollar bill, and tragically murdering him. This unspeakable act graphically displayed the inequality of police treatment towards people of color, incited protests as not seen in the US since the sixties and the tumultuous civil rights movement.

Millions woke up that day seeking the breathable air of true justice. This air is a goal to those of us who work every single day trying to make our world more equitable, inclusive, and tolerant. As we toil day in and day out to achieve this seemingly insurmountable task, we are continually reminded that we live in an imperfect world filled with amazing challenges.

Leading as a servant leader and teaching others to lead by example are two of the most powerful things we can all model for others. It was my mother, a person lacking a higher-level education, access to contacts in the upper echelons of society, or money and resources, who made me see for the first time that we all have the power to change the world for the better.

That is why I chose to honor her in this book. And what better way to do it than through her teachings and recipes, some of which I reproduce in her own handwriting as a visible testament to what she did for me and what she taught me to do for so many others.

All the recipes published here I've tried myself, sometimes modifying them; but, as *Mami* taught me, always being careful to deliver in each dish rich flavor and much love.

The secret ingredient is what brings to life any recipe. To me, food is a tool we can use to bring individuals together and share a special moment in which we unite people and cultures. I've lost count of the many times I've invited folks from all over the world to dinner parties at my home. To me, cooking is a generous act of love. I so enjoy it when someone tells me, "Your *tamales* take me back to my grandma's kitchen in the town I grew up."

As a contemporary Mexican woman, my mixed heritage is truly the fusion of two worlds: Indigenous and Spaniard (which in turn have been blended with so many more before they intersected). Foodwise, this unique combination has resulted in the global recognition of the diverse Mexican cuisine.

When I cook, I find harmony between the two worlds where I've lived most of my grown-up life. However, I know that learning how to use new ingredients and ways of preparing recipes is also part of what I must do to keep myself open to the beauty of everything and everyone in this world.

I'll illustrate this point with an anecdote: I've never seen yellow cheese in a Mexican dish before I moved to San Antonio, and was shocked the first time I saw that combination… but later realized that I was the one that needed to accept that this was part of another cultural fusion resulting in Tex-Mex cuisine. When I did, I understood that everything in life evolves, complementing at times and having to adapt other times.

Occasionally I'm asked what's my secret ingredient. I always answer "Love." When my children were little, I pretended that I sprinkled something magical on each dish before serving them. They would ask, "What are you sprinkling?" And I would answer, "It's my secret ingredient, love. But don't tell anyone, this is our secret." They always believed me, and even as teenagers they'd always asked me to sprinkle love on their dishes.

The use of secret ingredients translates perfectly to the way we evolve as leaders, and especially as persons trying to make the best of their lives. Personally, it wasn't until I found my place as an executive of diversity, equity and inclusion that I fell in love with my career. And, I know, it may take long for each of us to find our secret ingredient; but when we do, the combination with our unique qualities will produce something powerful, almost magical, allowing for everything to change for the better.

Ángeles Martínez Valenciano

Mami (Ana María Sánchez Quiroz) and Papi (Jesús Martínez Gamez) on their wedding day.

18 ## Barquitos Mexicanos.

Ingredientes
½ kilo de masa
150 grs. de harina
1 huevo
sal al gusto
2 aguacates

Modo De Hacerse
Se revuelve la harina con la masa la clara y la sal a que quede una masa compacta se extiende con el palote se forman los moldes propios de barquitos y se frien en aceite o en manteca bien caliente se deja hasta que dore y se rellenan con salmón guisado en jitomate frijoles con chorizo picadillo y se adornan con queso aguacate y una frita

Dreams Gone in Smoke

*"Don't you ever do
good things that appear to be bad
or bad things that appear to be good.
Instead, always try to do the things
that need to be done,
the way they need to be done."*

    To understand where a person comes from, where they think they are going and in what direction the rest of us see them moving, it is essential to go back, roll the flashback like in the movies, take a trip to the past exploring the events, people and culture that made them who they are today and take a good look at what brings them happiness, what they fear, what they love and what they abhor.

    All of us are a product of everything we've lived throughout our journey as human beings. We become a package carrying our history, stamped and labeled along the way.

    This is my story… and the story of how I lived all my experiences and got all my labels…

    My name is Ángeles Martínez Valenciano, I was born in Chicago, Illinois, but raised in San Luis Potosí, México. My favorite labels today are "mother" or *"Mami"* and "National Diversity Council & Global Diversity Council CEO". Of course, that was not the case my entire life. Before I got to this point, I had much to learn and even more to walk.

    My parents arrived in Chicago in the late 1960s. They were newly married and decided to take the plunge and become immigrants. My mom gave birth to me there, so I was a US citizen from the beginning. Only decades later was I able to appreciate the gift my parents gave me with their own sacrifice.

After arriving in Chicago, my parents moved to a predominantly Polish neighborhood and found employment. People in the neighborhood immediately resented their arrival and began a racist campaign to force them to move elsewhere. Sadly, decades later these practices continue today, and people in minority communities are still subjected to vicious acts of hatred while the authorities ignore these incidents or look the other way. As a result, people are now protesting, seeking justice and civil equality for all. Protests have become a crux of life in the United States.

My father bought a used car, a clunker as they are often called, so that he and *Mami* could drive to work. One morning, my father went outside and found his car going up in flames. He returned home and spoke with my mother. "I don't want my children to grow up in an environment where there is so much hatred, where there is so much evil, where there is so much cruelty. I don't want them to grow up thinking this is normal," he said.

At that moment they decided that even though they did not have much money, being newly arrived immigrants, they were going to return to México, even if it meant losing everything they had worked for. So, we did exactly that. We went back to San Luis Potosí, and my parents did not try to settle again as a family in the United States until their grown children found a path to return to the country where they were born.

I was a young child when all of this happened and had no recollection of the incident. That is until the day my father died. After I was given his belongings, I opened his wallet and found a faded photograph of a completely incinerated blue Volkswagen. On the back my dad wrote: *"Chicago 1969 - My dreams gone in smoke."* When I read that I instantly understood why they didn't stay in the United States.

Today I look at my past and I consider it a blessing that my parents decided not to stay and live in the United States.

And although this episode was subtly bequeathed to me, this event and all that I learned from my parents —and especially from Ana, my mother— gave me wings and the impetus I needed to launch myself into the difficult arena of diversity, equity and inclusion.

In retrospect, the Poles who burned my parents' car to a crisp, could never have imagined that one day their daughter would change the narrative of the story by dedicating herself to creating minority awareness so that other immigrants never have to experience what happened to her family.

Betún:

½ kilo de azúcar
1 tazo de agua como un cuarto

Se pone a hervir sin menearlo, de moverse mucho el punto es que se toma un poco y se moja en tantita agua y cuando truena que no sea demasiado poroso de punto, pero siempre que truene. 3 claras de huevo batidas a punto de turrón se les exprime 3 limones, ya estando de punto el azúcar se vacía a las claras batidas y se mueve rápidamente y al mismo se le pone el jugo de limón y luego se forra el pastel y se puede poner coco.

A Magical Town

"As long as you have beans,
rice and tortillas at home,
you have a meal."

I had the most wonderful childhood growing up in San Luis Potosí, my favorite place in all of México. I always tell my children that the town where I was raised is a magical town. So many cultures and styles converged in that place! Walking down any street you could find yourself standing before a building with a Baroque influence or a magnificent church from colonial times. Other times, you encountered gardens that seemed transplanted from Paradise itself. More than once I was transported back in time by the presence of the ancient cultures of the area. Being there was a real treat!

Our family was not wealthy, but we never considered ourselves poor. What we lacked when it came to money in the wallet, was more than compensated by the abundance of love, laughter, hugs, delicious food, time to play and time to help with home chores, friendships, and family unity.

My parents, my brother, my sister, and I lived in a small one-story house, with three bedrooms, one and a half baths, and a small patio in the back.

My dad, who in his youth had been a professional baseball player in México, worked in the fields in the United States as a *bracero*. We only got to see him when he was able to come home. But when he was there, we felt his presence as he was extremely strict with all of us.

We lived in a working-class neighborhood where all the men went out to work every day and the women stayed home to do housework and take care of the children. My father was frequently away in the United States and money was always in short supply, so my mother also worked. The truth is that my mother loved working and she excelled at running her own businesses. She was gifted when it came to connecting with anyone and everyone. *Mami* always found the key to people's hearts. She would figure out how could she help each one, she'd listen with the heart and would be able to say to that person whatever he or she needed to hear that day. Her intuition, her empathy and her deep understanding of people were keys to her helping others.

During the day she worked in her photography studio. Her passion was artistic photography, but she did whatever they asked her to do: school photos, passport or driver's license photos, business calendar photos. She never said "No" to any request, and she found the way to make everything happen. She was also a nurse, helping people who needed medical care at home. *Mami* was a *veladora*, which meant she worked the night shifts taking care of patients while the family went to sleep. She'd take care of all the patient's needs, including giving them their medicine or even an injection.

When I think of *Mami* I can always see her doing something, creating something, working on something, writing something. When I go through my memories, I can't find a single image of her where she's not happy. She was always smiling, cheerful, making jokes. She was always bringing joy to everyone in her life. Even though she had so many obstacles in her life and so much responsibility, *Mami* was always as chirpy as the forest birds in a Disney movie. At that time, Mexican culture was still very traditional. It was not "normal" or "good" to be a mother with children and a mostly absent spouse. Even though she was married, people gossiped about her "situation" behind her back. No matter what was said, or the horrible things people whispered about her, her attitude was to disregard the nonsensical gossip and focus her energy and attention in leading her life the way she wanted to lead it, keeping her eyes on her goals and objectives. *Mami* was extremely strict with us because she didn't want us to ever go astray. She gave each of us chores and tasks around the house to help her. Doing what she asked us to do showed us the value of teamwork and kept us from having too much spare time to get in trouble. That's how I learned to cook from a young age.

We didn't have much furniture at home and whatever we had were pieces that someone gave my mother as a gift or as payment for some work. But what *Mami* really loved was to collect religious-motif paintings. If I saw her coming down the street carrying something, I already knew it was Catholic in theme: the painting of a virgin, a Madonna, the Pope, Our Lady of Guadalupe. My mother was a prayer warrior, always talking to our heavenly family, but the one she liked best and taught me to love with all my heart is Our Lady of Perpetual Help. To this day I have a painting of her, which *Mami* gave me, hanging in my home.

My mom didn't have a car. She had learned to drive while living in Chicago, but she had an accident, and after that never wanted to drive again. To commute she would take the bus or a taxi. When she left the house, early in the morning, she was always dressed in a two-piece suit, jacket and skirt, like someone who dresses to go to an office. I never saw her in a nurse's uniform, nor did I saw her in jeans or T-shirts. She would always say that you were judged by how you looked and dressed. "Respect yourself and others will also respect you. If you show respect with your choice of clothing, people will treat you with respect," she would say as she was getting ready to go out. Even when doing basic chores and tasks, like go talk to a teacher at our school, she always presented herself in a professional manner. And what was like a miracle to me is that she made her own clothes, often using what she had and making it contemporary.

My mom would often practice what she preached. One great story that comes to mind to illustrate this point is the time when the military band played for her. In high school I always earned high grades. I was not the smartest student and did not possess a prodigious photographic memory, I studied a lot. One day I came home happy because I had gotten the best grades in the whole school; and in México when that happens you are chosen to be the flag bearer during the color guard on Flag Day. On that occasion, the event was to be attended by Mexican President,

Miguel De La Madrid Hurtado. "It's going to be my turn to carry the flag and I have the opportunity to take a picture with him," I said to *Mami*. "You have to go take the picture yourself," I asked. Of course, my mother did not have credentials from any newspaper or media outlet, but she had a fabulous presence, was very pretty, and dressed well...

We had little time to pull it off, so she went to work on it immediately.

That day we arrived at the Main Square, or *Plaza de Armas*, in San Luis Potosí filled with thousands of people awaiting the president's grand entrance. I was wearing my school uniform. My mom and I started to walk towards the stage. But before the stage was an area safely secured by several platoons of soldiers assigned to protect the president. They allowed me to go through, but when they saw my mom, they stopped her. I turned around and thought that they were not going to let her pass and that she was not going to be able to take the photo I so badly desired. My mom signaled to the soldier standing before her, she leaned forward and she whispered a few words to him. He gestured to let her pass and said, "Come in, please." When I saw that I thought, *I wonder what she told him to let her go through?!* And when I saw that they sat her in the front row, I almost died of emotion. Ultimately, *Mami* got to meet and greet México's President, kiss and hug included, and took his picture with me. When the event ended, I asked her what she did to get the soldiers to let her come to the VIP area. She adjusted her hair and with her unique charm explained to me, "Oh, my darling daughter, the soldier told me that I could not come in because I did not have my credentials. I replied that how was that possible as I was the director of the blablablabla preparatory school. When he heard that he apologized and let me through." Then she made a serious face and added, "Always, always, no matter where you are, always try to dress in such a way that people will give you respect because they see that you dress in a manner that commands respect." That's a lesson I have been able to personally validate many times during my professional life. People treat you depending on how you dress, and how you present yourself. She always understood that in order to achieve your goals, *"You have to dress according to the part you want to play."*

Her other business was her photo studio. Some of my early lessons from the professional world came by observing *Mami* run her shop. I remember being upset when digital photography started to become prevalent, as I realized that it could negatively impact my mom's livelihood. I told her that it was possible that her career as a photographer could be over as now anyone could just take a picture and print it on their own. She said to me, "My lovely daughter, competition is good and welcomed. I know that people will still come to me when they need a professionally taken photo. And I know I will still be able to charge them what I charge and make a living." She was right! Soon after, she also jumped into digital photography and was extremely excited when she realized that not only could she take photos at the studio, but now could also shoot other types of photographs, such as landscapes. Later in life, she took countless pictures in the United States and México; and when she travelled, she'd told us that she was on her artistic tour. Her darkroom is still in San Luis Potosí, just as she left it, even with the last photographs she left there.

Even though my parents worked a lot, we were always strapped for cash. Sometimes, we didn't even have enough money for food. But *Mami* would say, "As long as you have beans, rice and *tortillas*, you have enough to eat." The most amazing thing growing up is that we always had guests at our table, even though we couldn't afford it. And when she saw me worried, she'd say, "Don't worry, add water to the beans and we'll be fine." That way she always taught us that it's more important to give than to receive.

One of the most beautiful sayings of *Mami* was, *"Don't you ever do good things that appear to be bad or bad things that appear to be good. Instead, always try to do the things that need to be done, the way they need to be done."* Later in life, I understood this was the way she lived her life as a true Christian Catholic and it made me want to be more like her.

36

Bolitas de Berlanga

Ingredientes
1 lata de jamón endiablado
1/4 K. de papa
50 grs. de jamón
150 grs. de chorizo
2 huevos
1 cuchara de maizena

Manera de Hacerse
La papa cocida se muele
(se prensa) y se agrega al
jamón el chorizo desmenuzado
y frito con un pedazo de cebolla
se agrega también, se revuelve
todo y se hacen en forma
ovalada o bolitas por separado
se bate el huevo a punto de turrón
agregándole una cucharada de maizena
se envuelven las bolitas en aceite
o manteca bien caliente se sirven

A Family With Values

"Whenever you find yourself facing obstacles, whenever you feel that you can't do something, remember the lineage you come from: strong women, women that'll fight till the end."

I remember that period of my life as one of much learning, especially in the sense of getting to know my family deeply. It was particularly important to my mother that I understood where I came from, who I was, and who were the people that came before me. San Luis Potosí is in Central México, but *Mami* was from Durango, to the north. Her way of seeing life was different. When I asked her why she had gone so far from her mother, her brothers, her family, she answered, "Because in life you have to follow opportunities." The opportunity for her was to get married and start her own family. For her, her family was us, her children, and her husband.

Nevertheless, *Mami* insisted that it was extremely important to always remember my roots, my lineage, and my heritage. We were poor, but that didn't mean we had to feel ashamed. Quite the contrary.

Ours was a large and incredibly strong family that sought solace and refuge in their Catholic faith. My grandmother on my mother's side became a single mother of ten children at the age of thirty. My grandfather eloped with another woman and abandoned her. Their infant daughter at the time was only one year old. My mother used to tell me, "When you run into obstacles or feel like you can't do something, remember where you come from and who you come from: strong women, warrior women." Both of my parents came from families of ten children each.

My grandmother grew up during the Mexican Revolution. She said that churches were closed during that time because the regime insisted on the separation of Church and State. The priests had to perform the sacrament of marriage secretly, sometimes even in remote caves. If anyone found out, it would be bad for them. My grandmother got married as a girl, at fourteen. At fifteen she was already pregnant. That was the norm back then.

My name is Ángeles, same as my grandmother. She had to become mom and dad from a young age. She was strict with her children, but especially with her daughters, because she was worried that if they went astray or did something wrong, she'd be accused of being a failure as a mother and the one to blame for whatever her children did. Society is changing, but until recently it was a woman's responsibility to keep her family together and walking the righteous path. If a woman's husband divorced or left her, it was her fault. If he left because she couldn't take his abuse, it was her fault. If she couldn't bear him having another family or a lover, and he left her because of her crying, it was her fault. A woman was always in fault for whatever her man did to her. That is why my grandmother did not let her daughters go to dances or parties in town, for example. She was constantly afraid that they were going to elope or that someone would impregnate them. Even at a young age my mother disagreed with that way of thinking, and all the rules that were biased against women. My mom, being the oldest, was the one who assumed most of the responsibility for her brothers and sisters since my grandfather was gone. At that time, the oldest children were the ones who raised the youngest, and so my mother became the mother of her own siblings.

The most amazing thing about my grandmother was that despite the challenges she had to face, she managed to get all her children to finish school and then go on to college. And she was so proud of the fact that all her children were good people and none of them had ever committed any crimes. Grandma was strong and brave. Her favorite saying was, *"If lemons fall from the sky, take the opportunity to make some lemonade."* No matter what happened, instead of wallowing in despair she'd find a way to fix it.

My grandmother, my mother and even myself (to a certain degree) lived in a *machista* México were everything was supervised and approved by the man of the house, be it husband or father. A woman could have a college degree if her father allowed her to attend a university and gave her the funds to do so. She could travel if her father gave her permission. Even her partner in life had to be approved by her father.

My mother was as strong-willed as my grandmother, with tremendous faith and the wisdom to face any challenge that came her way. "Having faith is not just having faith in God, because God is with you, He is in you. To have faith is to have faith in yourself," she always told me. "When you have faith in yourself, you have faith in everything else and in a creation." She looked at everything with a heart filled with gratitude. From a very young age, she taught us to be grateful for everything. If the sun has risen, say, "Thank you, God, for the sun."

Mami was very caring and thoughtful for the little birds that came by our home. One day I noticed that some of them made very strange sounds. When I asked my mom why they were making those noises, she answered, "It is because they are thanking God." And when I asked her how she would know that, she replied, "Well, who else are they going to be thanking? Thank you that I can sing, thank you that I can fly, thank you that I can be." That was her starting point: always feeling gratitude for things, be they good or bad, those are the things that touched us and we must see the opportunities in them. That's exactly what she told us every time something happened. In other words, she could find the positive in everything. Her chirpy personality and endless positivity were sometimes difficult for the rest of us because living with someone who sees the bright side of everything can be a bit annoying. When we felt that my mom was going to start with her stories and her life advice, my sister and I would frequently look at each other and rolled our eyes… And now I am like that with my children… and I even tell them the same stories!

My middle child, Diego, says that his grandma was the female version of Saint Francis of Assisi, because she made dog, parakeet and cat live in harmony. I smile when I hear him remembering his grandmother like that... She found the true formula to always live positively.

My mom and the family weren't ashamed of being poor, but I was. I felt ashamed because I believed that if any person worked hard and studied hard, great achievements and income would follow. So, I couldn't understand why that was not the case for us. I felt sad because of our situation, especially during my teen years, which was the time when I most wanted to have new things, to be able to go out, to get a special haircut... It made me sad because I saw how hard they worked, how hard they tried to get ahead and could never achieve it.

I started working at a young age, when I was fourteen. I was very thin, tall, and I braided my hair to go out. I was finishing high school and working at the same time. It was then that I saw first-hand the importance of helping and contributing at home. Because I worked, *Mami* could relax a little more and did not have to rush to different jobs as she had money coming from her eldest daughter.

It was a wonderful childhood and youth. We had many traditions in our town. I especially loved serenades. Even today, I love that every May 10th, Mother's Day in México, throughout the country, moms are serenaded. If you have a boyfriend, that boyfriend must serenade his mom and then yours as well. The serenade can be performed with a *mariachi* or a *rondalla* or with a *estudiantina* or with a *trío*.

In México everything and anything is a reason for partying and giving thanks. It's always been like that. Growing up, it made me feel that I lived in a bubble of joy. It didn't matter position, income or health status, all of us were constantly celebrating life and everything it gives us... and even what it takes from us. Like the time our uncle had a heart attack and we made him *mole*. Everything is solved with food and music and good *tequila*. And, of course, we always did it together, each one brought something so that the responsibility never fell on a single person. It was something different when I arrived in this country and I saw that each one paid for their own, without family or friends supporting them with anything. In México everyone contributes to the party.

For the *quinceañera*, for instance, you have a godmother for the cake, another for the dress, a third one for the music, and so on. As for food, the unique dishes of each family are welcome at each celebration.

Mami on her way to work.

37

Budín "El Reloj"

Ingredientes

½ K. de papa
½ K. " zanahoria
1 manojo de acelgas o espinacas
6 huevos
100 grs. de mantequilla
125 " " Crema
50 grs. de queso añejo
1 latita de Chile morrón

Manera de hacerse

Las acelgas cocidas se muelen, se ... con mantequilla agregándoles un poco de crema, la tercera parte del queso, sal y se dejan desecar, se colocan en un molde engrasado, se ... sobre esta se pone la papa y sobre la papa la zanahoria, la papa prensada

Ahead of Their Time

> *"Alongside a great man*
> *you'll find a great woman.*
> *Not behind him. Not before him.*
> *By his side."*

    As kids growing up, we always saw our parents as the most amazing, most united, most romantic couple we've ever met. We never heard our parents argue. We never heard them fight. We never heard them using angry words. We never saw them in an altercation. If they had their moments of disagreement, we never witnessed it. And this led us to believe that all couples were like that, even the ones we would be a part of in the future. It turns out that what we saw was not the norm but something unusual. And that's why I always told them that they created an unattainable expectation, be it in romantic as in social and professional relationships.
    My siblings and I didn't realize this was the case until we had our own love interests and spouses. There was this one time, when we were all adults and having lunch together when my brother said to my parents, "My sisters and I were talking, and we couldn't find a single memory of you guys being angry at each other or fighting. Not one. How can that be possible?" My parents looked at each other and smiled. Then my mother replied, "Do you remember all those afternoons when your father and I disappeared because we told you we were going to buy bread?" We said, "Yes." *Mami* confessed, "It was then, on those walks away from you kids, when we did tell each other everything. And we did it that way because in our families our parents fought a lot and something that

we remembered too much from our childhood and youth was the screaming. So, when we got married, we promised ourselves that we would never fight in front of our children."

Even though this was a good thing for a developing child, it ultimately left me without a clue on how to fight without thinking that it's the end of the world. I have no concept of how to do it right. In example: When I had disagreements or discussions with my ex-husband, I made them worst in my mind than they really were. Everyone argues, everyone gets angry, we all have differences, but not having a tool to accurately measure shades of outrage damaged my ability to properly react, communicate and resolve problems during challenging times.

I brought that deficiency to my workplace. When someone disagreed with me or pointed to a fault, I took it very seriously and immediately jumped to the conclusion that the trust had been broken forever and the relationship had come to an end. I made everything too personal and got deeply hurt every time. It took many volatile instances for me to realize that there is more than one way to approach problems without burning everything, including relationships and opportunities. I realized I could have disagreements, even arguments, that could be resolved without necessarily damaging or even influencing future interactions. I remember how hard was for me to train myself in recognizing nuances and being able to identify different levels of escalation and how to lower the intensity and reach agreements.

This is not something that I learned immediately. It took years of practice in real life.

Many times we end up torturing ourselves for nothing. We carry the weight we place on issues that potentially did not mean as much to the other person. On top of that, as a Latina I know now how different culturally I am from people in the US. Back then I found it shocking having an argument with someone at work one day and that same person talking to me the next day, even inviting me for coffee, as if nothing happened. I was very confused and took adjustment on my part to accept that others and I were not always going to agree and be on the same page, but we could work together and even develop friendships.

Aside from the fighting issue, my parents modeled many greats things for me. One of the most important lessons I learned from seeing them handle life was that even though they endured economic poverty they managed to always be at peace, with each other and with the world. For example, my mother never had words of resentment or contempt toward my father. She never said something like, "Your dad promised me the moon and the stars and look where we are." She never complained about not having material things or enough money. At that time, women would get married and the husband was supposed to be the sole provider. It was not like that for her. She always had to work but she never complained —the truth is she enjoyed being active, so maybe that helped her.

Today I truly appreciate the fact that *Mami* was never afraid of facing new challenges and trying new things, even if ultimately things didn't turn out the way she hoped they would. If she thought of something she wanted to do, nothing would stop her. I would ask her, "Are you going to try? What if it doesn't work?" Her answer was always the same, "God willing, it will work." This is a phrase that stayed in my heart and that I say to myself constantly. Life is about making decisions and taking risks, but if we ultimately give it to God, peace will take over us and we will know that what happens is because God wants it to be that way. As a mom, I teach my children to face life the way *Mami* taught me and my siblings, and I also say to them what she said to us, "God willing…"

Even at a time when people didn't speak about diversity and inclusion, my mother fought for minorities and those being different to be included. On one occasion my mother and I went to a conference at the university where I was studying. A doctor was giving the talk. He was an extremely *macho* man, one of those people who needed all the praise to be directed to him, and for the world to revolve around him and no one else. Back then it was the custom in México that when you invited someone of that relevance, you always invited his wife, and she would sit near the stage close to the main speaker. *Mami* and I were sitting in the front of the auditorium and engaged with everything on stage. At one point he said, "As it is well known, behind a great man there is a great woman," and looked behind, where his wife was sitting, while pointing to her. At that moment *Mami* leaned over to where I was and whispered, "Idiot. He's an idiot. Alongside a great man is a great woman. Not behind. Not before. By his side. Never forget that." It was at that moment that I understood that I was equal to any man. If I wanted to study engineering, if I wanted to study computer science, if I wanted to study programming, her declaration of support helped me understand that nothing should prevent me from doing what I wanted to do as a woman. That no one should dare limit me, that no one should dare ask her why I was studying for a man's profession instead of becoming a teacher or a nurse, the traditional careers for a woman at that time. It was so important for me to know that there was a person by my side who always knew, even before me, what I was going to achieve and what I was going to do with my life. She believed in me even before I believed in myself.

I really learned from the best. She would never back down from a challenge. She'd always figure a way to reach her goals. She was our family's mind and heart. She was the center of our universe. She was always a very tender and loving mother, extremely sweet and effusive. I loved her hands, she always had them impeccable, her long nails manicured with neutral tones polish, her skin so soft. I remember her holding me by the hand, or giving me a kiss on the forehead, and doing it with so much warmth. She was a dedicated, self-sacrificing, and incredibly strong mom.

Because she spent the most time with us, *Mami* was the one that dictated the rules and enforced them at home.

Each one of us dealt with her way of doing things differently.

My sister was party central, she loved parties and was always invited to everything because she was the life of the party. *Mami* would say to her, "It's best if you don't go to every party, that way they'll miss you and they'll be happier to see you next time." But my sister was rebellious, she would tell our mother, "You are trying to make me into a nun." And then she would run to the bathroom, place a towel on her head, simulating a nun's veil, and start parading around, saying, "I'm a nun, I'm a nun, I'm in a convent." My mom would laugh but didn't change her mind. My sister could scream, cry, rant and rave. Mom wouldn't budge. "No" was "No" in our home. That's why my brother and I never argued with her once she said, "No." *Mami* was the final authority, and we knew to respect her. If we didn't behave, mom didn't have a problem using *la chancla* (a house shoe, like slippers or flip flops) to punish us. On the other hand, dad only needed to raise his voice and that would be enough for us to stop in our tracks.

With Mami at the conference that I mention in this chapter.

Buñuelos de Viento

Ingredientes
1/4 de harina
1 cucharita de anis
2 huevos
4 Cucharadas de azúcar
1 vaso grande de leche
1/4 de manteca

Manera de Hacerse
Se baten las claras a punto de turrón, agregando las yemas, enseguida la harina y el azúcar; en una taza se pone a hervir el anis con agua, despues que este frio se le agrega lo anterior, se le pone media taza, enseguida se le pone la leche hasta dejar una pasta como atoler.

Always Do Good. In Every Instance, for Everybody

"Enjoy what you have.
Do the best you can with what you have.
Always help others. Always.
Remember that your prize will come later, not in this
world. Help without expecting anything in return."

By observing my mother's behavior, I learned from a young age how important it is to be inclusive and to develop empathy for everyone. She was always looking for a way to help whoever she saw in need. Sometimes, it was something as simple as inviting a friend, a relative, even a stranger, to eat at home. On other occasions, she would be the first one to lend a helping hand whenever necessary through her photography or nursing jobs.

Even though she had so little to give, in terms of material things, *Mami* was incredibly generous. I learned an amazing lesson from her on this subject when I was in my teens. Years later I understood this prepared me for a similar situation close to home.

My brother had a friend named Javier. He was twelve at the time and his parents were divorced. He lived with his dad, who was abusive. Since Javier was at my house a lot, my mom sort of took him in and became the mother he didn't have, since his own mom abandoned her family for another man. Javier was like a brother to us and a fourth child to *Mami*. He'd be with us most of the day but would go to his own house to sleep. One year, on May 10th, Mother's Day in México, Javier arrived at our home as we were getting ready to celebrate. A few minutes later, Javier's father showed up with his fiancé and said to Javier, "Get in the car, we are going out to celebrate my future wife this Mother's Day." To which Javier replied, "I'm already celebrating with my mother. She lives in this house." That was the exact moment Javier became *Mami's* son. And she treated him exactly as she did with us. If he misbehaved, he'd also get the *chancla* as punishment, just like us.

Even though we had to survive with only the basics, I remember my home as a welcoming place, and my growing up there as a warm and peaceful time of my life.

I've often wondered how was it possible that having so few resources my mother was such a happy person. We could feel it in the way she behaved, we could see it in her face and her chirpy personality. It didn't matter if things were tough, she always had a word of encouragement, she was always friendly, I never saw her disappointed or down. She was a person who loved life. She was a person who never complained about the wealth of others. She was a person who set a goal, kept moving forward, without looking to the sides, without complaining, without comparing herself to others. Living like this helped her make of her life what she wanted. And yet she always told me, "I want you to achieve everything that I could not achieve. I want you to study. I want you to have a career. I want you to be remarkably successful. I want you to travel." She never traveled, but she liked to read a lot, so she always told me about certain places that she would like to visit one day.

I have an image etched in my mind and in my heart. It was the first time I called *Mami* to tell her that I was traveling for work and that I was going to Brazil. She was deeply happy. As soon as I arrived at the hotel, I called her. She told me, "You are my eyes. Explain to me in detail what you see." Immediately I started telling her about the place where I was, my room in the hotel, the beach beyond my window, the weather... All the details I could find to share with her. It became a tradition that every time I traveled somewhere, I'd call and describe everything to her. She'd be so excited and always repeated to me, "You are my eyes to the world. To a world I never knew." Over time, I became particularly good at describing every detail to her. We spent hours on the phone talking about all the places where I had to travel for work. I was still young, I was not married or had children. And the most incredible thing is that I could share the world with *Mami* who never voiced a word of envy or felt a hint of jealousy. She genuinely enjoyed living all of that through me.

It was then that I realized that there are different types of mothers. There are the mothers who want to live through their children and do everything possible so that their children do what they want them to do, and to somehow feel fulfilled. Then there is the mother who may not have been able to achieve all the things that she would have wanted to achieve in her own life but who feels incredible gratification when she sees her children succeed. And she never harbors bitterness or resentment toward her own child for doing better than she did.

Best of all, my mom was always quick to bring me back to Earth if she suddenly saw me becoming a tad haughty because of my career achievements. She would say to me, "Much taller towers have fallen. Nothing is safe in life, nothing. Enjoy what you have. Do the best you can with what you have. Always help other people, always. And remember that your reward will be given to you later, do not expect to ever receive it here, in this world. Help always without expecting anything."

Cajeta de Camote

Para 1 Kilo de camote, 1 litro de leche y medio de azúcar

Modo de Prepararse

Se limpia el camote y se pone a cocer, luego se muele en metate y en seguida se cuela hasta que quede como atole, luego se pone al fuego con los demás ingredientes se les dá el punto de cajeta y se quita, luego de sacar del fuego le ponen nueces picadas, pasas, coco rayado y también se puede agregar piloncillo y se adorna cada platito con la mitad de una nuez.

Painful Transitions

"You should always be looking out for the opportunities."

It can be said that it was an accident that I was born in the United States. It was something that happened because at the beginning of their life as a married couple my parents decided that they wanted to make a life in this country, a dream that they quickly had to give up because they did not see how they were going to raise their children in the hostile environment, especially towards Mexican immigrants, of the 1970s.

Having been physically attacked emotionally scarred *Mami* and *Papi*, altering forever their perception of what this country stood for, to the point of wanting to leave it behind as a place to raise a family.

But life is interesting. Sometimes it forces us to take a second look at our own biases.

Shortly before I graduated from my hometown university with a bachelor's degree in Computer Science and Business Administration, I was offered the opportunity of a lifetime: an all-paid internship at General Electric in the United States.

When they found out, my parents were terribly upset. They couldn't believe that after the horrible way our family was treated, I was considering going back to the US.

"This is the worst news ever! We left that country, which treated us so badly, because we did not see that there was going to be an opportunity for you, and everything was so difficult for us there. And now you want to go? No, *Negrita*, that is not going to happen," said my mother, distraught that I was mulling over an offer that would place me in a country that she feared would hurt me.

Then my father said, "I am so happy... so proud of all that you have achieved here in your own country! Pursuing a career and working at the same time you completed your studies. You found a way to pay for everything, be it thanks to the money you earned with your hard work or the scholarships you were granted to cover your tuition and other expenses. Why would you want to leave if you are in a great place right now? You're now a professional that can accomplish a lot in México. Why go there, to the US? Maybe you won't make as much money if you stay in your country... but what happens when you leave here, and you end up failing there?"

Both started painting my future life in the United States as a horror story. My dad was the harshest, listing non-stop all the bad things that could happen to me. And even though my father was not a *machista* and never opposed me getting a professional degree, he also threw in the mix the classic saying, *"Respectable ladies do not live by themselves."*

I was beginning to feel I would never be able to do that internship, when all of the sudden my parents tossed me a lifesaver as they said, "The only way we can allow you to go is if your brother goes with you."

Given that my brother, Jesús, had already decided he would soon leave for Texas, I was almost positive my first hurdle was taken care.

But I knew that my father would keep coming at me to try to stop me. It was not my parents as a block, just *Papi*. *Mami* was noticeably quiet. I later realized that my mom was on my side but that she remained silent to allow my father to speak his mind, and even let him believe it was he who had the last word on the topic. In the end, it would be my mom and I that would come to a decision together; after that, she would convince *Papi* to say "Yes."

Later in life, when I understood what she did, I learned to apply her techniques when negotiating with male colleagues.

Knowing my dad as well as I did, I decided that in the next three months, the time left before college graduation and the end of my contract at my current job, I would continue to try to convince him whenever and however I could.

During that time my mom approached me to request a private conversation between the two of us. "I have already decided, I am going to go. I have an opportunity to do an internship in my chosen industry, which is computing. It's six months; and from there, if I can do this job and get this engineering certification, then I can go to work building computers and doing many things within computing, which is what interests me," I said to her. Once we talked, mom took it upon herself to convince my dad.

Not only did my mom help me leave, but also covered up for me so that my dad didn't find out that I had gone alone to Kentucky. The internship was with General Electric in Louisville; I got accepted there because the company where I worked in San Luis Potosí was a subsidiary of GE in México; it was them who recommended me. Meanwhile, my brother settled in Laredo, Texas, looked for work and began his university studies.

Being born in Chicago provided me with my US citizenship, but I will always self-identify as an immigrant because I had to face the same challenges as anyone else who comes from a foreign country.

One of the first challenges I had to face from day one in Louisville was my English. I spoke it with a very heavy accent, and so many people think that having an accent means that person must be intellectually deficient. This is not true at all, especially for those of us who learn a second language as adults. We know intelligence has nothing to do with language acquisition! Yet I endured so many harsh, hurtful remarks and criticism because of the way I spoke.

At any rate, I thought I knew English when I arrived here, but it was not enough, and it was not the colloquial language I needed to survive and thrive on a daily basis. I didn't speak or write it at the level I desperately needed. To make matters worse, every time someone spoke to me, I was very afraid, anxious, nervous, because for me they were speaking very fast, just like when they say that we speak Spanish too fast, that was exactly my impression. When they spoke to me at work for my different projects in

English, I was extremely nervous. I'd listened to them speak almost without breathing and I sometimes did not understand what they were saying.

Because my main language is Spanish, I think first in Spanish, I do the mental translation and then I speak. To understand, I first listen and then translate into Spanish. This is not a simple or agile process to new arrivals in a country with another language.

It was then that I encountered the wicked Wild Male Syndrome for the first time in my life. The fact was that the other engineers, all white Anglo men, constantly complained about my presence during our classes and labs. They surrounded me like a pack of ferocious wolves and told me as a group, "Because of you, because you don't speak English well, because you can't read it well, many classes are running longer than they should. You ask a lot of questions. Why don't you go back to your country? Why do you want to be here if you are a burden? Why are you here in the first place and how did you get here? Just go back." But they weren't going to run me off. There was no way I was going to go back to San Luis Potosí and say, "I failed." That's when I decided to turn this problem into a positive challenge. The more they said to me, "You can't," the more I replied to myself, *Watch me. Just Watch Me. Give me some time and you'll see me doing everything you do... and better than any of you.*

So, I dedicated myself to learning English. At night, instead of sleeping, I would read the textbooks that we would use in class the next day. Not only did I read all the material in advance, but I would practice in front of the mirror the pronunciation of the words we would use. This is how I learned to give myself the same opportunities as others by being able to read, write and speak in English. This is an exercise that I have had to continue doing throughout my life, since there will always be new topics and words that I do not know. Today, I still find it extremely disappointing when large groups of people are brushed aside and labeled "not as capable" because of having an accent. I can see that we need to continue to challenge everyone to take a good look into their biases. Think about it... Most often than not, individuals with accents have mastered not one but two or more languages.

While this pressure kept me on my toes all the time, whenever I spoke with my parents on the phone I painted an optimistic picture for them. I couldn't share what was really happening to me. If I had, they would have told me to come back home. That was not what I wanted. I already had in mind that as soon as I finished my internship in Kentucky and obtained the Microsoft Certified Systems Engineer certificate, I'd move to Laredo to be with my brother and start my professional life in the United States.

Cocono Relleno

Se pesa el cocono según los kilos que pese son las horas con que deben cocerse, a kilo por hora se unta bien de mantequilla sal y el jugo de naranjas se mete al horno ya con su relleno que ya se tendrá preparado de antemano se bolteo y se le dan baños con el jugo de las naranjas

Manera de hacersele al relleno

1 kilo de carne de puerco y todos los dentros se cocen con su ajo y cebolla, se muele todo y se guisa con mantequilla y se le pone nueces pasas y 1 kilo de manzana en pedacitos y aceitunas y pan remojado en leche salsa de tomate y si no hay salsa se le pone un punto de azúcar

Cultural Shock in Texas

"Always be yourself.
Keep in mind you are responsible
for how your life turns out to be,
that nobody should make decisions for you,
that you should always be independent."

When I finished my internship, I went to Laredo. My brother had not said anything, good or bad, about the city but I arrived there with high expectations of finding a welcoming place that would make me feel as if I never left San Luis Potosí.

Laredo was a small town, unlike my beautiful town or anywhere in México for that matter. The people there were vastly different from what I imagined they would be.

Basically, it was mainstream America and I had to face the culture shock of living there. Until that moment I had a sheltered life in the United States, one dictated by my internship's schedule, which did not involve dealing with the regular problems of daily living. Now, I needed to take care of all the things that legal immigrants must do when they arrive in this country.

First off, I did not know the relationship between my social security number and getting the needed credit for things I wanted to buy through a bank loan, such as a car. Social security means medical insurance in México, very different use of the same term as in the US. Because I didn't know this, I was embarrassed more than once!

Second obstacle, I needed to buy a car so that I had reliable transportation to go to work. I went to the dealership and explained to the salesperson what I was looking for. The salesperson said to me, "We need to check on your credit." And I replied, "Okay." He asked, "Well, we need your social security number and with that, we'll check on your credit and see if we can offer you financing." And I explained, "Well, I don't have a job at the moment." He then asked, "How are you planning to pay for the car if you don't have a job?" I thought my answer made complete sense, "Well, I need the car so I can find a job and, once I'm employed, I can pay for it." They immediately showed me to the door. I understood then that achieving my goals in the United States was not going to be as easy as I initially thought.

During those first weeks and months, when things were not going as smoothly, I started to hear in my mind everything *Papi* said to me before I left. *It's not going to be easy... They'll try to sabotage your efforts... No one will offer to help you... It will be hard for you to make your dreams come true... You're a woman... It's different for us over there...* But every time I had a setback, and I heard my father's words about me going back home and thought of me having to say to him, "I failed. You were right to warn me," my own stubbornness would emerge full-fledged and pushed me to regain steam and look only to the finish line.

It didn't take long for me to decide that Laredo was not my type of city and headed north, to San Antonio. In my mind San Antonio was a larger city with great influence of the Spanish culture and a large Mexican-American population... and because of that, it had to be a much more welcoming and relatable place for me.

I was twenty-three years old when I moved to the city of the Alamo. What I found was not what I expected.

I sure needed to keep in touch with my parents but because international long distance was still incredibly expensive, we decided we would talk only once a week and at a time of day were rates were cheaper.

Whenever we spoke, I'd say everything they needed to hear to believe that I was doing well, that I was learning many things, that people were friendly. I would tell them that people treated me better because I had a college degree. That I received much support and encouragement from those around me. Of course, all my words were a lie. What I was experiencing was nothing like that.

I would hang up from speaking with them and cried at least half an hour.

It wasn't until much later, when I felt the worse was already in my rearview mirror, that I had the courage to tell them the truth. I first told my mom and afterwards my father. When I was a child, my mother instinctively knew when something was bothering me just by listening to my tone of voice. She told me that when I started my life in San Antonio she was so devastated by her loss, by her knowing I was not going back to San Luis Potosí, she somehow blocked it all out so she couldn't hear the pain in my voice and that way avoided being further hurt herself.

Truthfully, they were agonizing as much as I was.

My sister told me about it one day. She said, "It was almost as if you died when you left. They'd cry every day." I replied, "No wonder I didn't do well. They were mourning me instead of giving me their blessing." It was a revelation to hear about their struggles. When I left, I thought I was going with my mother's blessing. The reality was that she supported me even though she didn't agree with my plans. Nevertheless, she was sad and missed me dearly.

Just knowing about all this, made everything even harder for me. I couldn't share what was happening to me. I never gave them any kind of trouble when I was under their roof, and it was not the time to start now. I decided I needed to take care of myself without anyone's help. I needed them to see that I was doing fine and was happy. Most importantly, I needed them to trust me and have faith that I'd reach my goals.

Before arriving in San Antonio, I thought this city would be Paradise to me. That I'd be surrounded by people like me and that I'd never miss my culture or my delicious Mexican food.

And, yes, at first impression it does look like the perfect place for a Latina like me.

Reality slapped me in the face soon enough.

I needed a place to live. Since I didn't have a job just yet, it occurred to me that I could make do by having roommates with whom I could share costs. I had my life savings and some leftover earnings from the GE internship to help me cover the first months. I looked in the classifieds and started calling people who had a Hispanic name. I expected to be received with open arms. I was hoping that I would be comfortable here, with people who spoke my language and appreciated our food.

Logically, if I saw that someone's name was, say, Norma Gonzales, I would call that person. And after chatting for a while, they'd always answered me, "I don't think we are a good fit. We would not match at all." Years later I realized that the questions I asked were those of a girl who had just arrived from provincial México, with a hugely different understanding of life from what it was here. I was very conservative. I wanted to know that there were not going to be boys in the apartment, that there were not going to be drugs, that there were not going to be things like that. I was asking for too much.

In the end, it was not Latinos who opened the doors for me, but Anglo-American people. I did not understand what could be happening! Was I on an episode of "The Twilight Zone"?

I was already desperate and downright frustrated when my first roommate in this country came into my life. She was Anglo and didn't speak a bit of Spanish. I told myself that living with her would force me to practice my English, which was extremely important to me, so I smiled and looked forward to the opportunity that presented itself in such an unusual way.

That leap into the void spun into a great outcome after all. And I made the most of it, so I came out ahead.

The apartment had only one bedroom, so we bought two single beds and shared the small space with her two cats, the incredibly spoiled Sebastián and César. At least the pets had Latino names!

It was my roommate who also helped me get a job with an authorized IBM agent, working on their computer networks. It was something incredible, because she and I moved to the apartment on a Saturday and by Monday I already had the interview. They hired me immediately.

When I started working, I was making less than about twenty thousand dollars a year. It was the mid-1990s, but it was low pay for someone with a college education and a certification. I tried not to even think about that, but instead focused on the fact that I finally had a job where I was going to put everything I had learned into practice.

And I loved it!

I was doing the configuration on the IBM AS/400 computer network system for medium and large companies. This was an innovative system that was strongly entering the market and that can still be seen in some hospitals today.

Remember computers with a black screen and green letters? Well, those were the ones I installed.

As distributors of IBM products, it was almost like we were employees of them since the company took care of giving us all our training and education.

We were a team in charge of sales, installation and maintenance. Sales representatives were always Anglo. They always made an incredible amount of money since they received a commission from the hundreds of thousands of dollars our clients were billed.

I clearly remember a visit to do a presentation at a hospital. We were gunning for a super juicy account. The salesperson made the presentation corresponding to the sale, it was he who represented IBM with the solution. But it was me, the technician who earned a pittance, who made all the pertinent recommendations and then would oversee the entire process, including configuring the systems to maximize the usefulness of our products and services within their organization.

We drove back and forth from those appointments in fancy cars: Porsche, BMW, Mercedes Benz... And I was speechless because I knew that these luxuries came from the commissions they earned thanks to my effort. But I was not envious of them; what I wanted to know was how I could get to be behind the wheel, like them.

That never materialized for me in that company. But I'll always carry with me that (weird) image of not seeing anyone who looked like me in the management offices of that important company that did business in that city full of Hispanics. What I observed was something that taught me a huge lesson and prepared me to be the woman who today fights with all her might to create diverse, inclusive and equitable work environments at all levels.

While I was there, I dedicated myself to continue learning English and to excelling in my job. I wanted to move up the corporate ladder, but not because of materialism *per se*. I admit that I am a person who likes to have beautiful things, but at that time my goal was to be seen by my colleagues as an equal. The only way to achieve that was by showing them that I was up for any challenge and that I was able to accomplish as much as any of them. Of course, I also wanted to make more money so I could send home the monthly amount as I had promised I'd do, a tad more if possible. I lived in the United States but never forgot what it is like to live in poverty and lack basic necessities.

I stayed in that job because of my need to learn and to receive a steady income. However, the longer I stayed there the more I saw things that I thought were not right. I soon realized that many would come to me when they had technical difficulties or difficult questions, but I was taken for granted since appreciation or inclusion, or even a "Thank You," were never part of their behavior.

At first, I thought that this was how "weird" they were with everyone, but then I discovered that I was the only one who was treated that way. They made me work hard and long, and then they hid my achievements, as if I had not contributed, as if I did not exist.

One of the hardest lessons was given to me by a woman who worked as a sales representative. At twenty-three years old and being quite naive, I thought that if someone could help me move forward in that place it would be a woman.

One day I approached her, asked her to help me learn everything I needed to know and do to get to her position. I didn't have the right word for that concept then, but now I know I was inviting her to be my mentor. She said to me, "Of course. I will gladly help you. But we would do it when no one is watching, because that is something that should not be done here. You have your place and I have mine. But you are a good person and I like to support women. So, I'm going to guide you the way you want, but you can't tell anyone. We are going to do it during the moments when we are alone. For example, when I'm reading your configuration results. First, I am going to ask you to make the configuration of seven organizations to which I am going to send this information. And when you finish giving me all this, we start with your course to guide you."

When she replied with such kind words and a real plan, I was grateful and excited. I'd think to myself, *Now I'll learn from someone who knows how to speak to the client, how to make an appointment, how to make a sale. I'll be able to achieve what I want.* I would imagine myself as a successful businesswoman, being able to invite my parents over to San Antonio, going to pick them up in my own car, taking them to my apartment. I wanted them to see that their *Negrita* made it in this country.

I gave this woman what she wanted for the seven companies in the record time of two weeks. Normally such a project takes at least two months to complete. But I was able to finish it much quicker by neglecting my sleep. I kept telling myself that the faster I delivered what she asked for, the sooner we would start my lessons. I also believed that the time I saved her on the projects would become extra time she'd spend on my training. I was on my way out of the lower rung of employment!

When I gave her everything, she said, "Hey, in two weeks you have all this ready? Are you sure everything is okay?" I replied, "Yes. I've already done all the tests on our computers here. Everything is ready." Then she told me that she would verify what I gave her before making the appointments and that after all that we would start with what she promised.

I was happy. Positive that this woman would help me; and now with more enthusiasm because I had done a good job for her.

And yet, while I felt high on hope, she stabbed me on the back. Not only did she go to speak with Human Resources to ask for my transfer to another department, but she also told them, "These technicians are looking at us as if we are stupid. This girl comes from a university that probably doesn't even exist, because nobody knows if she really has a college education. She finished a project in two weeks, when everyone is finishing the same volume of work in two months. You have to move her to another team. She can't stay here." And when everybody learned that I had completed the configurations for seven companies in two weeks, the whole world turned against me. They never considered that to achieve this I've been working twenty hours a day without rest. The other techs got upset with me because my speed made them look bad, like they were lazy.

That situation hurt my soul, but it also taught me a lot.

On my way out to the department to which I was transferred because of this woman, I got brave and confronted her, "Why did you do this to me? Why did you go say all this? Now nobody in the team of engineers or the team of technicians talks to me. And they are upset for a good reason: they have to divide their time between their families and their work; while I, who am single and young, can work overtime and complete setups in less time. Didn't you think of that?" And she answered me something that I will never forget, "It's because you proved that your people are lazy. What you did makes me understand that you people can do it... you just don't want to do it because you are all a bunch of lazy people."

That was her answer. That we (Latinos) are lazy, because everyone could do what I did in record time, but that we take our sweet time to extend the projects because we are lazy!

And she ended her argument by saying, "I don't want to work with a person who is lazy or who is not honest."

That was a huge lesson for me. Within an organization there will always be politics and struggles, people will take sides, some will look at you and see a good employee and others will want to bring you down for whatever reason. But I think that for people like us, women, women of color, Latinas, there is always that additional barrier and burden of carrying all the stereotypes that society has placed on our community or our various communities.

Let's look at Latinos. Some of the stereotypes attached to us are: Latinos are illegal aliens (a term meant to dehumanize people who entered the country illegally, and even legally, especially people of color); Latinos come to steal our jobs and take advantage of our generous system; Latinos don't speak English; Latinos do field work but there are no professionals in that group; Latinos can be entry job employees, but they should never be managers or leaders; Latinos are cheaters; Latina women are only good for cleaning, cooking, and sex; Latinos don't pay taxes but they love welfare... Most people have no idea how tough and frustrating it is to fight to prove our worth at the same time we disprove all these labels!

That day, when I was leaving the office, they notified me that they were going to move me to another department. My heart skipped a beat when I heard that. It wasn't what I wanted. I loved my job, I had been there for three years, and I wanted to keep moving forward to sales and business development. But the decision had been made and I was to change teams or leave the company.

I walked with my head up to the parking lot, sat in my car and cried thick tears for an hour. I felt sorry for myself, I asked myself with sadness and anger, *Why is it that no one can value the work that I do? Why does everything have to focus on the fact that I am Mexican? Why can't they just say that Ángeles did this right or did this wrong? Why does it always have to be Ángeles, the Mexican, the minority, the brown, the immigrant?*

I know, it's hard to remain cool, calm and collected when injustice shows up. It was hard for me. But, while we cannot control the behavior of others, we can control our reaction, even to evil deeds. We can look for the silver lining and say to ourselves, *Everything happens for a reason*. When we do that, we can see opportunities even when we are falling.

I have learned the most valuable lessons when I have been wronged, used, or when I have faltered in my own choices. I didn't see it while crying in my car that day, but if it hadn't been for that woman who tried to damage me career wise, I wouldn't have had the chance to develop to the fullest of my potential from that point on.

It was serendipity that the department they transferred me to was in charge of sales of IBM products and services in Latin America. Coincidentally, the Internet had just began to emerge throughout the world and became a familiar place for people outside of the technical field. It was also when many of the installations began to be carried out remotely. The cherry on top was that my new manager, a white man, was a person who not only gave me the opportunity to work close to him, but said to me, "You know? There is something in you, I see something in you. I believe that you have to be one of the first people in this company who should go to Harrisburg, Pennsylvania, to do the training on this new Internet platform."

And I was.

It was an incredible experience to be in Pennsylvania. It broadened my cultural horizons. I did not understand who the Mennonites were, for example. I had heard the term, and recognized that this group of people existed, but I did not know they were there. I got to know them a little. That experience taught me about the many ways of celebrating God and what's sacred. Also, since my training took place during the winter, I was delighted I got to see and touch the snow.

I applied myself and learned everything available regarding configurations in the new technical environment. When I returned to San Antonio, the team was ready to learn from me everything that I had learned. I did a Train the Trainer program with my teammates. Later, because of being fluent in Spanish, I was sent to train our colleagues in México, and then to Chile, and then to all the places where IBM had operations in Latin America. And it was at that moment that I saw the opportunity to not only make use of my Spanish, since I was bilingual, but to excel in the work I was doing. I had observed that at the company's annual conference they never gave awards to minority women, and that made me realize that I would have to do my best, and much more, if I wanted to shine above everyone else.

It was then that my new manager surprised me when he said, "You know? Several branches are requesting that I send you to do their training. But before that, I want you to start thinking about what you want to do in the future. I want you to be the person that in the future will inherit my position. Or, if you prefer it, I want you to be the person in Human Resources who launches and manages the Training Department for the entire organization in Latin America. Those are your two options. Which one are you going to take?"

Before making a decision, I called *Mami* and told her about the two proposals I had in front of me. She told me very lovingly, "Whatever you decide to do, you know that you have our blessing. We are joyful for what you have achieved so far, which is something incredible. The only thing I want from you is that you never forget where you come from… And, furthermore, never forget that every time you have the opportunity to achieve something, you should lift other people with you." What she was telling me was that in the same way that someone had given me the opportunity and saw the raw talent in me, that I should always do the same.

I decided that I would be taking charge of Human Resources and all the training in Latin America, which at that time meant an incredible expansion for the organization. I assisted with establishing teams in all the other countries. Millions of dollars were made in business and new jobs were created.

That was the first time I had a decent and good salary. I was finally able to buy a new car, the white convertible Mustang of my dreams, and invite my parents to San Antonio, to my own apartment. It was the first trip they made to see me, and they stayed with me for a whole month.

I remember their look of pride when the two of them arrived at my apartment. The pride they had of being in that space, of meeting my friends and seeing where I worked. They were already beginning their retirement years and it was such a joy to show them my accomplishments and reassure them that everything was going well in my life.

Recetas

Encanelados

½ Kilo de harina
300 gramos de azucar
¼ cucharada de sal
¼ Kilo de manteca
2 huevos
3 cucharaditas de Royal

Se bate el azucar con la manteca hasta que espese luego se mezclan los huevos enseguida la harina con el Royal y la sal.

Se hacen bolitos del tamaño que se desee se mete al horno y se envuelven con azucar y canela

An Immigrant's Experience

"If you want to be the boss, the one that gives orders, you must first know how to do things yourself and know how things work."

When my parents came to visit me for the first time, I came to the realization that I wouldn't be returning to México. The pain of understanding that as a matter of fact hit me hard. Every immigrant confronts that experience in a unique way. For me, it was unbearable. It was almost like I died emotionally. I knew that I was not going to return to the place and the people I loved with all my heart and that my life, for at least the next ten to twenty years, was going to be lived in this country.

I was grateful for the opportunity, but it meant separation from my family. This is the price immigrants pay to make a life in the United States. It doesn't matter how you came to this country. The cost of taking that decision is pretty much the same for every immigrant. We all give up so much to gain access to the possibility of having a better life, which in my case was a professional career. People outside of our circles have no idea, no clue whatsoever, of the sacrifices all of us make. Instead of empathizing with our plight, outsiders judge us in a biased way. Whether you entered the country legally or illegally, it doesn't make a difference, you'll be most likely deemed as someone undeserving of being in the USA. That's the struggle and it never goes away. Even if you've lived for decades in this country and have been incredibly successful, you'll be treated with suspicion.

There's a famous metal sculpture of a man who has a hole in the middle of his body. He represents the immigrant who left his country behind, his family, his believes, his traditions... And the void with which he lives his entire life as an immigrant. I saw the sculpture and immediately understood its powerful message because I feel the same way all the time. Much of me is missing.

Even as I was in deep pain, I knew I didn't have time to waste wallowing in self-pity, I knew I had to work, I had to have the discipline to say to myself, *I cannot let my emotions overtake me.* It would have been easy to say, "I'm leaving. Let's see how I'll do that, but I'm leaving because I can't stand it anymore." I missed my parents and my family so much that it would have been a very easy thing to do. But as I often say to my sons, "Things that are worthwhile take sacrifice and love." So, I stayed, and I am to a certain degree at peace with that decision. I have seen many others pack up and leave. People who couldn't stand it and threw in the towel. I don't blame them. Especially with the constant animosity towards minorities. There are times when I also wonder, *Was it worth it?* And I really have to tell myself that even with all its flaws, here I have a better quality of life and everything I need for myself in the future.

I believe that all those emotions stemming from being an immigrant always remain within each of us. The most significant is that sense of not belonging here or there. When I go to México I feel comfortable, but with everything I have missed in so many decades, I have become somewhat of a tourist in my own country. And here, in the US, I can't shake the impression that people are still looking at me as if I had just arrived.

However, the last time I was in México with the Women in Leadership Symposium, something quite strange happened to me. Something magical maybe. As I was deplaning, I physically felt that something in my whole being was changing, as if I was shedding all the unnecessary baggage I've been carrying around since arriving in the United States. With every step I took, I felt that every label placed upon me all the decades living outside of my country of origin —immigrant, woman of color, Chicana, Mexican American, Latina, Latinx— started to disappear from my mind and my soul. Suddenly I was Ángeles, a human being. I was Ángeles, period! It was joyful to find myself as myself, without the emotional and even physical burden of having to accept all those labels with which I really do not identify one hundred percent.

I think that was the reason why this symposium in México was so successful. The women who attended saw me as one of them, they identified with my story. I was the daughter who was returning to her country. They recognized that it was there where I belonged, that my essence was there. That it was there where I didn't have to carry the weight of the labels. That it was there where I could be myself and nothing else.

But upon returning to the United States, and becoming once again an immigrant, the first thing I felt was the weight of the labels.

There are so many reasons to come to the United States, many reasons why so many of us cease being completely ourselves and allow others to label us as they please.

The main reason, the reality that we want people who see us with such contempt to know, is that this is a country where any of us will find more opportunities to educate ourselves, develop ourselves, evolve, climb the corporate ladder, start a business, give flight to our passions, and even have a more comfortable life. Unfortunately, it's what we find and don't find in our countries of origin what propels us to leave. Why do people like me, educated and ambitious, have to leave to become someone, to be able to fulfill themselves professionally? It is because opportunities are not available to everyone in our Latin American countries. This is due in large part to the fact that corruption and being connected or "plugged in" prevail in the places where we come from. If we see that no matter how hard we try, there is no hope... If we know that without "patronage" or "nepotism" there is no way forward... If we recognize that the mentality of crushing those who try to shine corresponds to an endemic evil... We will have to accept that our beloved nations will continue to suffer a talent exodus.

Real talent will always find an opportunity somewhere.

However, it's sad to realize that after giving up our own true selves in exchange for a second chance in the United States, it's things like racism, discrimination and inequality that will keep distracting us from accomplishing what we came here to do.

Labels like "minority," "women of color," "immigrant woman," place us in lesser categories. They carry a powerful message, somehow letting the world know there's a deficiency, that we do not belong in the same playing field as others.

I don't want to be discriminated because I'm an immigrant, Latina, women of color. But, by the same token, I don't want anyone to think I will demand special treatment. I just want to be recognized on my own merits. I just want to have equal rights and responsibilities, as everyone else.

I want to be hired because I'm recognized as high level talent in my field of expertise, but never because I'm in a category that a company needs to hire to fill some sort of diversity quota. I want to get a bank loan because I qualify, but never because there's some sort of law that makes the bank give me more credit than I can handle. I want to be able to choose for myself where I want to live and not to be redlined based on my race or ethnicity. I want to be treated with respect by the police and other authorities, and never to feel unsafe because of the color of my skin, my name or my accent. I just want to be able to be myself, to live in peace, to develop professionally to my capacity, to breathe easily wherever I am and whoever I'm with.

Unfortunately for me, what I want is not my reality.

My reality is that many times over the years since I arrived in Louisville I have stopped and asked myself if it's worth continuing to live and work here. I have even doubted if I belong or if I am an impostor, if I'm playing a role that is not mine to play.

Truth is that after so many years of hearing that we do not belong, that we should not be here, of banging our heads against the walls of limitations imposed by society, of always seeing and hearing negative things about immigrants and the people of our Latin American heritage... There comes a time when those limiting ideas that others have hung on all of us immigrant Latinos like chains that prevent each of us from moving with the agility that we know we have, begin to permeate our minds and our hearts until they make us believe the lies we've been told about ourselves and our community. And we change and we grow in sadness and resentment and become different people than the ones we were when we arrived.

It's like someone engraved in our hearts the phrase we often hear and feel in our entire beings, "You don't belong."

I remember going to a bistro in San Francisco for lunch. It was a small restaurant, barely ten tables, but rather elegant. I had just made a presentation to a group of executives, and I decided to go to dinner by myself. They sat me down, but fifteen minutes later no waiter had showed up to take my order. I saw that the diners at other tables already had their glasses of water and that wait staff came to take their order and leave the breadbasket. It was almost as if I had become invisible. Frustrated, I tried to stop a waiter that walked by my table. "Excuse me, no one has come by to take my order," I said. He looked at me, turned around, and continued walking. At that moment I didn't feel rage nor anger, no, I felt shame. I turned around and looked at everyone looking at me in the bistro, there was no empathy in that room. Embarrassed, I picked up my things and left. I knew they were not going to serve me.

Unfortunately, I've also have had these kinds of experiences with people from other minorities, including Latino immigrants and Latinos born in the United States.

They were incidents I never expected to happen with those I thought were in the same boat as me.

I think it is even more painful, more traumatic, when it happens with someone who looks like us.

It is something that has happened to me in San Antonio. I've already learned to deal with it; but when I first arrived, I experienced some confusing interactions with the people in that city.

San Antonio is a city with an impressive Spanish and Mexican heritage. It is also a lineage club for the descendants of those who founded the city or have lived here for centuries. Only third, fourth, fifth, sixth generation Mexican in the United States are allowed in the group. Recent or new immigrants, even if they are Mexican, don't fit. "You are not one of us. You don't have our experience," feels like they are saying.

I couldn't understand it.

How is it possible that I, being a Mexican and an immigrant, would not be accepted by generations of Mexican

Americans who have been here before? Little by little I discovered that it is the mentality of the "only scraps economy", of "there's not enough for everyone. Therefore, first I serve myself, my family and my friends" way of thinking that leads to making those people who should shake hands with us do not even acknowledge our existence. My son Diego has a name for them: "The ones who close the doors to ensure that no one else comes in." They are immigrants and descendants of immigrants who arrive, achieve, and then do not want to share. They believe the opportunities are only for them, and they feel upset when a new Mexican girl, like me, comes to "steal" what is theirs.

The circle in San Antonio is made up mainly of Mexican Americans who arrived long time ago or who have been here for a long time and thus have lost their cultural essence. They do not speak Spanish, they do not cook authentic dishes, they do not know their history, their music and their literature, or even have a true connection to their home country. These cultural deficiencies are due both to the number of generations that have passed and to institutional racism in American education in the last century, where children were not allowed to speak Spanish in schools and where, as a survival method, those who could pass as Anglo would hide or change the immigration history of their family.

I remember the first time I heard that they were celebrating something called "Fiesta." I said, "Yes, that's great! This is something very Mexican." I was joyful and so delighted, trembling with expectation when I went to celebrate with them. But I was terribly disappointed upon arrival since the whole thing was not what I expected but a watered-down version with none of the flavor you'd find in an authentic "Fiesta". Over time I heard quite a few stories about what this celebration really encompassed and how the concept of each piece of this event had been forged. It was then that I understood that it is not that we have nothing in common, but that this "Fiesta" came to be through the use of cultural appropriation, which takes the parts of our culture easily recognized and palatable by mainstream society and packs them in in such a way that they seem to represent our Mexican culture, when in fact it's a fairly diluted version of who we are. The same thing is now happening with the most beautiful tradition and celebration of "Day of the Dead".

Many people do think that it's better to have something that represents us, as Latinos, for public consumption than to have nothing. My point of view is that inclusion means to include everything and everybody in the mix. I do love this city where I've made a life and raised a family, but I'd love it even more if we would allow others to see us as we truly are, and not as this "commercial version" of us.

The first time that I went to a Mexican restaurant in San Antonio, I almost fell off my chair when I tried their food. The dish I ordered had cheddar cheese! You'd never see this type of cheese in authentic Mexican cuisine! I didn't say anything since I didn't want to offend anyone and make enemies right away. I just thought to myself, *Maybe this is the way they prepare Mexican dishes in Texas, like some type of blended cooking.*

Same happened to me when it came to literature. I couldn't understand how people there didn't worship our world-acclaimed Latin American writers, such as Octavio Paz, Laura Esquivel, Isabel Allende, Juan de Dios Peza, Amado Nervo, Gabriela Mistral, Pablo Neruda, Mario Vargas Llosa, Gabriel García Marquez... and so many others traditionally representative of our culture. It just blew my mind!

One way to understand why I and so many immigrants are not appreciated in places where a "Latino culture" has already been established by those who came before us is that we make them look bad when they somehow offer this manufactured culture, and we show the true culture of our countries. This creates a conflict as we are "invading" their space, destroying their marketing, taking them off the pedestal.

Whatever the reason, the people who looked like me were nothing like me and their willingness to help was non-existent. The truth is that the people who supported me the most during my career were Anglos. It's not exactly what one would expect, but it happened. It pains me to say it and I know that I will receive a lot of criticism for these words. However, it is important to expose the truth of what we observe so that everyone, including myself, has the opportunity to change and improve.

This is my truth; and in the face of this reality, I decided that this vicious circle would end with me. We have to be aware of what truly goes around us and accept reality if we want to make real changes. What happened to me continues to happen today. When I speak with Latino immigrants from different countries of origin and from diverse socioeconomic levels, many tell me their stories of disappointment with our own community. They describe how much it hurts to be treated with contempt by those who should be welcoming them and showing them the way. That is why today it is a priority for me to give immigrants an opportunity and ask everyone to have more patience and understanding towards those who are going through all the difficulties that integration into a new culture entail. I can also say that the reason why I decided to write this book originally in Spanish and later translate it, was to emphasize how difficult it is to learn another language, and at the same time praise and give voice to our Latino immigrants who do so much good for this country.

Women in Leadership Program, United States.
This program, which I started seventeen years ago, has now reached over one and a half million women leaders in the United States and countries abroad. The topic of leadership is one that I am passionate about, it has given me the opportunity to meet and share with great leaders around the world.

The sculpture of the emigrant by artist Bruno Catalano in Marseille, France. A man with a suitcase full of dreams leaves his home in search of a better life. The space in the chest represents the emptiness of leaving behind everything he loves.

Ensalada de Atún

Ingredientes
1 lata de atún
1 lechuga
2 cucharadas de mayonesa
1 tomate grande

Manera de Hacerse

Se pica muy bien la lechuga y el tomate por separado. Se desmenuza muy bien el atún poniéndole las 2 cucharadas de mayonesa, se revuelve bien agregándole la lechuga y el tomate que tenemos ya preparado, se revuelve todo muy bien y se sirve en frío.

1/2/62.

Sharing Recipes, Connecting Hearts

*"Every ingredient is important,
but not every ingredient has equal value...
some will be necessary and others complementary.
And to top it off you need to add something surprising,
something unique and original that will make the recipe yours."*

At the beginning of my immigration journey in San Antonio I felt very lonely. I was by myself in a foreign country, working my way in a foreign culture. I didn't have any family or friends by my side, which made it much harder. Pretty soon, that loneliness turned into a longing for connecting with places, people and culture where I felt a sense of belonging, especially with my mother.

When I finally started to make friends in San Antonio, I observed that many of them didn't have great relationships with their mothers. It made me appreciate so much more the strong bond developed between Latinas and their mothers. I also found it strange that many people here preferred to see their families only for certain events, such as Thanksgiving, and not every day of the year, as we Latinos love to do with our families. I don't need specific dates to enjoy my family, to want to be with them, and I'll never see it as an obligation either. For us it is an honor to be with our family, to enjoy daily life together. I missed so much our Sunday family gatherings in México!

My heart ached for my family and my culture, but I didn't want that yearning to be my excuse for leaving the United States.

It was around this time that I started calling my mom every day. Since I had a good job, I could finally afford the cost of international calls. One of the things that gave me the strength to cope with those feelings of emptiness and loneliness was that when I called *Mami* I asked for her guidance in preparing the dishes that she made for us when we were growing up. I wanted real Mexican food, not the Tex-Mex flavor that to me was not a representation of our country's unique cuisine.

It was during those conversations about food preparation and recipes that, through her positive words and unavoidable wisdom, my mom also gave me the courage to keep going. The preparation of those dishes became my lifeline.

Sometimes it was difficult to find an ingredient, or I did not know how to translate its name into English. So, I would seek mom's advice again. And while we talked about recipes, she always found a way to turn the cooking class into a life lesson.

When I was not sure if I would be able to get certain ingredient, like *flor de calabaza*, she would tell me, "All ingredients are important, but each ingredient has a value; so, if you can't find the exact ingredient you have to look for something similar. Do not despair, you can always use a substitute. Of all the ingredients you will need, some will be seasonings. That means that not everything is going to be a priority. And it is also important to find the element of surprise, something that gives your dish its uniqueness. That way, when you put everything together, you will create something that will be an original."

This piece of advice has a lot to do with leadership. Each person is an ingredient. We all contribute something different. Sometimes we will be a condiment and, other times, the most important part of the dish. There are people who will give the element of surprise, there are people who will add flavor to life... I quickly realized that I'd greatly benefit by applying those concepts to my daily professional life. And the most important part was when she told me: "The blending of the ingredients is what makes the dish superb." That is diversity for me.

Throughout all those lessons I'd hear my mother's voice and immediately felt better. We laughed so much while cooking together at dinner time. I ate like a queen and learned from her how to be patient and how to get a hold of my own emotions. While guiding me through food preparation, *Mami* shared with me everything I needed to know about leadership... She was better than any college professor!

I talked a lot with my mom about being aware of who we are, having compassion for the people around us, having an attitude of service, treating everyone with respect, and living life with humility. We now understand this as having emotional intelligence. These are qualities that we look for in the leader who wants to serve, or servant leader, rather than one only wanting to elevate themselves. I learned a lot from her. Here is a woman who did not travel outside her country, who was not educated in a great university, but who had immense wisdom. As a mother she gave so much of herself; and, without knowing it, she was preparing me, she was teaching me all the values that I would use in the future. Her kindness taught me generosity. What I learned from her also had to do with her faith. She focused her life on the principles of Christianity, such as service, humility, and always giving and supporting each other. I didn't have to go to a class to learn any of that, I was lucky I lived it through the examples she gave me every day of her life.

One of the things that helped me the most during that time of transition and adaptation, after I first arrived in San Antonio and already knew that I would stay in the United States, was to find a way to be diplomatic about what I observed to be Mexican and that to me was clearly not. I had to tell myself that the different ingredients and spices used in Tex-Mex cuisine were tailored to suit the local palate and at the same time educate others about what's true Mexican cuisine and what's not. Point in case: México has thirty-two states, and each state has a traditional dish, a *taco* is not a traditional dish anywhere in México. *Enchiladas* are another example. I know how to make twenty-two versions of *enchiladas*. On top of that, each state has its specialties; in some regions it can be very vegetarian, in others it is meat, in others it is fish and seafood. That's not what we find here. Food that is known as Mexican in the United States has almost the same ingredients — beans, rice, avocado, meat, some sauce, and tortillas— adapted to local taste.

Mami always insisted that a recipe must evolve. She also was adamant that when she gave me a recipe, I needed to make the recipe mine by changing ingredients or modifying its preparation or adding something unique. She would be unwavering about the fact that each one of us must do their own version of things, so that we leave our mark on everything we touch.

By the same token, she'd tell me that because each dish is prepared by a unique and special human being, the result will be different from one person to the other. She was really telling me what Heraclitus had stated centuries ago, *"You can't bathe in the same river twice."* Recognizing the truth in the words of the philosopher can give us an advantage in our daily life and help us recognize why everyone, every moment and everything matters.

One evening I told my mom that I would work hard and become a busy executive who would not have time for cooking; I just wanted to learn right away so I could eat every day what I liked. And I told her that I would hire a cook from México to make me my favorite dishes. And she answered me, "Look: to give orders, you first have to know how to do things. Because if you don't know how to do things yourself, anyone can tell you that they did what you asked them to do, but you will not know if they did it well or not because you don't know how to do it." That was another lesson for me.

My mother also passed on to me her love for reading. She'd prefer the writings of strong women, like Sor Juana Inés de la Cruz, Alfonsina Storni, Juana de Ibarbourou, among many others. And because she had eclectic taste when it came to choosing books, I learned to be eclectic as well.

Mami was always an admirer of strong women, but she never resented any man. She was a strong woman and she told me that I would be too, "Always be you. Keep in mind that you are responsible for your life. That no one should decide for you. That you must maintain your independence. Don't wait for someone to do things for you... least of all a man. When you do things and make decisions, you should always be yourself and not someone's wife." She was very much in love with my dad, and he encouraged her to be herself. They were the perfect combination.

I have in my garden a small bench where the two of them always sat in the afternoon, together, holding hands, praying the rosary. They had serenity, love, and strength. They were never offended by what the other brought to the relationship. I have not been able to find love interests that behaved in that life-affirming manner. The partners that I've had in the past were not able to bear the weight of what I've achieved and the goals that I've set for myself. It seemed to me that they didn't like me to shine more than they did.

When I found my voice, when I discovered my value as a person, as an executive, I had to sacrifice other things, I had to put everything on the scales and decide what I'd give more importance to: Have a steady relationship or a relationship where I had to clip my wings to make things work for him. Being a mother or being an executive. Those decisions were exceedingly difficult. At the beginning of my career, I was clear that I did not want to have a family because I wanted to focus on developing professionally. I wanted the opportunity to achieve set goals, to travel, to see the world. And I didn't see myself as mom. Of course, it is impossible to recognize myself in that statement today. Being a mom is the most important role in my current life, the one I love and treasure the most.

Each generation of women had to determine what they stood for and what was that they valued. And each generation has done things differently. I feel like my Gen X was the one that somehow got the message that we had to choose, that we couldn't have it all at the same time. That creates stagnation for women. In my mind I saw myself married, but at 40-45 years old, after a career full of achievements. Even as a young adult my life plan was completely off the chart for a Mexican woman, who was "expected" to be married and with children in her twenties.

54   "Gallina de Frijoles"

Ingredientes
1/4 de frijoles
100 g de queso
2 cucharadas de harina
unos chiles en vinagre

Modo de Hacerse
Se ponen a cocer los frijoles
con sal, cuando están bien cocidos se escurren y se muelen agregando un pedazo de cebolla, bien
molida y un ajo, se pone la manteca
en la lumbre cuando está bien
caliente se fríe la harina cuando
está dorada se agregan los frijoles
que tenemos preparados se dejan hervir
a que sequen bien, poniendole en medio queso
fallado se envuelven se le dá la forma de
una gallina con un chile rojo se le forma la
cresta un pedacito de queso se le pone los ojos
el pico con un pedazo de lechuga se adorna con
mas queso rallado y unos chiles.

Climbing the Corporate Ladder While Starting a Family

"Every time you have the opportunity to achieve something make sure you share that achievement with other people."

The beginning of my career in Human Resources at JP Morgan Chase marked the end of my engineering career and a new start in a professional world that turned out to be perfect for me. From a totally technical profession I moved to an area of talent development, diversity and inclusion. And it was thanks to that leap that I had the opportunity to participate in many leadership courses, both internal and external. It was an important goal for the company that its employees had access to all the education opportunities they offered. I loved that I was able to take a leadership course every three months!

I started working as a human resources manager and eventually became an assistant vice president of global diversity. Under my leadership we created programs in Latin America, Canada, and part of the United States. We were also able to complete the first integration of the Call Center in Mumbai. In the year 2000 I took over the reins of the Fast Track for Women of Color program, which identified the most talented women of color who were ready for leadership in the company and placed them in rotations in a variety of positions providing upward mobility through cross training across different aspects of the business.

I met my ex-husband, Tony, a few months before moving on to my new job. We met at a conference. He worked for another bank at the time. Our love affair moved fast. He was Latino but fourth generation Mexican, which means that he was quite different from me. By the time I realized this, we were already sharing a life. A year later I got pregnant. I had just started my new job at JP Morgan Chase, I had so much to accomplish, I had so much to learn. So, my first reaction was that this was not the ideal time for me to become a mother.

I soon changed my mind, recognizing that I was never going to be completely ready for that important role. So, if it was going to happen, it was better that it was then because I was with the person I loved, an incredibly good person, and everything I was looking for at that time.

Sometimes we think we know what we want. Truth is we don't really know what we want until we have it. For me, becoming a mother to Tony, my first child, was the greatest gift I could ever receive in my life. I never imagined having to undergo so much physical suffering from pregnancy in order to give life to a human being. I was only thirty years old, but it was a very risky pregnancy. When I held that baby in my arms for the first time, I felt so much love... I never imagined that I could love so much. At that moment the Ángeles who had her entire life planned and her professional career organized in detail felt compelled by love and happily rerouted. In that instant I knew how loved I was and how much I loved that child.

Mami was by my side throughout the delivery, along with my first friend in San Antonio, Rebecca Wilkins, who remains one of my best friends to this day. It was a very painful natural birth, that thankfully went well. When my son Tony was born the doctor asked who was going to cut the umbilical cord. My husband said he would do it himself and came over to get the scissors. At that moment *Mami* looked at me and looked at Rebecca, then she said, "Do you know what this umbilical cord is? It's the source of life between mother and child throughout the pregnancy. If women were a little smarter, and more honest, and kinder to each other, we would realize that we have much in common, not only the fact of being women but also that we have the possibility of giving life, and therefore this umbilical cord connects us all as mothers."

It was when I became a mother, first to Tony and later to Diego, that I understood the importance of having a group of people who are in the same situation as us. Until then I had only worked with men, I had no women in my corporate life. From that moment on, I understood that I needed a group of experienced women who would help me cope and excel because my mother would not always be by my side. It was an important lesson. This is something that I see that greatly impacts the professional advancement of women. There is this attitude that because it cost me a lot to get there, it also must cause equal suffering to those who come behind. Instead, we should say, "You know what? It took me a long time to get here, but I did get here. Now I'm going to help you to move up as well; so that you can do it faster or more easily than me."

Mami stayed with me the first year of each childbirth to take care of my sons. The second year I did start to feel guilty because I had more and more responsibility at work, and it required a lot of travel. I felt bad leaving them when they were so small. Before I left, I would sit them by the window and show them the moon, then I would tell them how many moons it would take for me to get back home. That was the way they understood how long it was going to be until we were all together again.

As a mother working at an organization that demanded performing at peak levels all the time in order to achieve goals, I knew that it was very possible I would not be given advancement opportunities since it was assumed that because I had children, I couldn't stay later, I couldn't travel, or I couldn't take on responsibilities that separated me from my family. Sometimes we are not presented with opportunities, and we don't even know it because someone else made that decision for us. Women fall behind and wither when that happens to them. Mothers and, even worst, single mothers (which I later became due to divorce), run the risk of stagnation, but not because of themselves, but because others perceive that their circumstances are an impediment for development. I felt that to avoid being pigeonholed, I had to take every opportunity and do everything they asked of me, and do it better than anyone else, so that being a mother would never be an obstacle in anyone's mind. I carried the guilt of not doing my share of housework, of leaving my children, and of not seeing them. I carried the responsibility of doing everything to perfection at work or being left behind. On top of that, when I was married I had the added weight of a husband who wanted to be the most important person in my life. If he wasn't first in my life, then he'd find some other woman who would put him on a pedestal.

I was exhausted all the time. I felt like a robot. Giving, giving, giving. Living my life as a reaction to everyone else's demands. Never granting myself an allowance for much needed rest or "me time."

Today I can say that offering credence to the belief that women who are mothers should also be superheroes is problematic. The only thing we achieve by keeping that idea alive is giving ourselves more work and more responsibility. I feel that women are always tired, exhausted, because we believe that we must do everything by ourselves and without asking for help. If I could go back in time, there are things that I would not have given so much importance to, I would've tried to have a balance, to do what I had to do in such a way that I could have the same results without wearing myself out so much. But, at that time, it was important for me to give the impression of having everything under control, to paint the picture that everything was fine, especially in my work.

When I reached the highest level available to me at the time within JP Morgan Chase there were quite a few people who did not want me to be in that position and who told me that they assumed that I was there because I was a product of affirmative action, a token, a corporate nod, a symbol that expressed outwardly that the organization was inclusive, that it believed in the power of diversity. The problem I faced was that in the company there were career people, women especially, who had not advanced to that stage. They were the ones who showed resentment because in three years I had managed to climb remarkably high. And, of course, there were unfavorable rumors about what "I've done" to get there.

But every time someone doubts me, insults me, or underestimates me, it makes me want to prove my worth even more. *Watch me, look at me and you will see what I am capable of,* was what I thought to myself.

Soon enough I discovered that women need to develop that innate ability that men possess, where they can easily separate business from personal interactions. I was amazed when I observed them disparaging each other at a meeting and minutes later go out for drinks together. Women harbor resentment instead. For example, in the first company I worked, I felt bitterness when the same women were recognized year after year. There were no opportunities for anyone else outside of certain circles. With those sure bet outcomes, it was difficult for me to find the motivation to beat them since I sensed it was a fool's errand.

All and all, I have to say loud and grateful that my experience with JP Morgan Chase was excellent. I can't imagine having the career I had, with so many achievements and opportunities, anywhere else. I loved that they were so far ahead when it came to work/life balance, the harmony between career and personal life. A couple of advantages of working with them, as far as my children were concerned, was that they had a nursery in the same building where the office was located, and they also allowed us to take the children on business trips.

This was a time of great balance and of great understanding of the equilibrium between my professional life and my family life. For me it was a mixed bag. I was always trying to find new ways of having both my professional and family life coexisting in harmony, so that I would never lose a beat on either of them. I'd constantly asked myself, *What's the magic recipe to be able to incorporate all those ingredients in my life?* By observing and learning I managed to have great professional growth without having to sacrifice family life. That way I took every opportunity that was offered to me because I knew I had earned it.

Even though there were no Latina or immigrant women in leadership positions at my grade level, Anglo women were very generous with their time, with their advice, with their ideas, and with their guidance. From this wonderful time there are two people to whom I will forever be grateful, as they gave me their unconditional support: Mary Jean George and, especially, Phyllis Gallay. I took two lessons from interacting with them. The first, that it is necessary to create development opportunities to incorporate greater diversity at the managerial and authority levels. The second, when starting a new job, look for someone to model ourselves after and who will give us a hand.

In the most stressful moments, I like to take a break in the kitchen. Going back to my roots through the preparation of dishes is something that helps me focus.

With the loves of my life, my three sons: Tony, Diego and Mario.

10

Nopales Rellenos.

Ingredientes.

Se cortan los nopales tiernitos se lavan bien pelados y se ponen a cocer con sal y un pedazo de cebolla, un ajo y un tomate el orégano se puede moler o cuando está el chile guisado se espolvorea el chile debe guisarse con poca grasa se sasona con sal y ahí se ponen los nopalitos rellenos

Modo de Hacerse

Los nopales despues de bien cocidos se escurren rellenando con queso los huevos batidos a punto de Turón como para lam-

Dennis Kennedy, The Unexpected Ingredient

*"Anything that is worth in life
will have a price and a risk.
You must risk in order to find out
if the price was worth it or not."*

For many it's impossible to imagine that just as they make it to the highest step of their corporate career, they would discover their true passion and leave everything for it. But that's exactly what happened to me.

There came a time when I had no more steps to climb within my team at JP Morgan Chase in San Antonio. I was then offered the prize I longed for: an Assistant Vice President position at the headquarters in Manhattan, New York. My salary would be in the high six figures plus bonus, and the company would take care of the move.

At that time, I already had a fairly complete family: my husband Tony and my two sons, Tony and Diego. It was the year 2001 and I can say that it was an excellent idea to analyze the situation before being overtaken by how incredible it all sounded on paper.

Looking before jumping led me to realize many things while making the home search trip. The first thing was that although I would earn a much higher salary than I did in San Antonio, those six figures would not be enough for me in a city where the cost of living is as high as its skyscrapers. We would have had to live in Connecticut or New Jersey, and that meant I would spend a minimum of three hours a day on the train, which would add up to being away from home twelve hours each day, on top of all the time I would have to be on the road for work.

I took the job but told myself I'd think about it while out there by myself. The truth is that I was very hesitant about staying and moving my family to such a different place.

I didn't know what to do about our future as a family. Although my gut feeling was up in arms screaming that this job was going to rob me of more time than I was willing to give it up.

It was right then that I realized that my most important role in life was not my job, it was not being a wife, but a mother. My favorite title is "Mom." It is the one that I keep closest to my heart, it's the one I treasure. When any of us leaves a company, we are quickly forgotten, it's like we were never there. A husband walks away, files for divorce, remarries, turns the page. A son or daughter never leaves, they never forget who gave them that heart that beats in their chest.

I would be working in an international corporation, in an extremely high position, in Manhattan... I would be living the dream of so many, but I knew that in the long term the situation would be unbearable for me.

And then something unusual happened.

One day, before moving, my boss called me to his office and told me about this person who had been calling and calling him: Dennis Kennedy. He explained that he was having a hard time getting rid of him and asked me to take care of his problem. He requested me to speak to him as a courtesy, but to make sure he'd be gone forever after that.

I followed my boss's instructions and made an appointment. Dennis Kennedy came to my office. I welcomed him, as it is usually done in the corporate world, and he took the opportunity to present his proposal for his new organization, the Texas Diversity Council. He thought we could sponsor it, since JP Morgan Chase had just been named as the number one organization in Diversity by *Diversity Inc. Magazine.*

I remember him asking me if I liked my job. I told him that my position in San Antonio was going to be eliminated but that they were giving me a promotion to our headquarters in New York in a much higher position. He told me he'd love to chat with me a bit more, even if we met outside of the office. I answered him that I'd be happy to meet for coffee or something, but that he should call me directly instead of my boss.

We met later, we talked about his concept, what he wanted to achieve, the meetings he was having with large companies. I asked him for his business plan, and he replied that he had everything on his mind, but nothing in writing. I laughed. But he started to explain the details and tried to convince me of the value of his proposal. I had already said yes to the promotion. I was going alone for six months and would fly back to San Antonio on the weekends. I had concluded that that was the only thing I could do since I wanted to stay at my company. At that point I saw Dennis Kennedy as a dreamer and left it there. I had bigger plans.

I did as planned and went to New York City by myself. One day Dennis called me and said, "I know you have your job, but if you want to be at home with your children, I want to propose that you come and work with me. You can work from home. The downside is that I cannot offer you a salary just yet because the organization is not incorporated, we do not have the 501 (c) (3). But if you accept, we can start working. You have so much knowledge in all things related to diversity. I want to start a leadership program for women."

I could have turned it down and keep going with my own plans, but Dennis Kennedy touched something inside of me that sparked an immense desire to impact the community in a palpable way on a day-to-day basis.

Instead of going back and forth in my mind, I called my mother and, after explaining the situation I said, "I don't know how am I going to make this decision!" To which she replied, "In your heart you have already decided. This man needs you. What you are going to accomplish together is going to help so many people! You must do it. You have to go with him." I still had my doubts because I knew the lack of salary would cause my family a headache. She told me, "Everything in life that is worthwhile has a price and has a risk. You must take the risk in order to figure out if it was worth it or not. This is one of those defining moments in your life." It was she who convinced me.

It was the year 2003. I left behind my safe corporate job to follow Dennis Kennedy.

The beginning of that new journey involved many daily harsh sacrifices. We had to visit all these big companies, sell them the concept of what we were trying to achieve, have them write us a check, sign up for our programs, support us. Dennis met my one and two-year-old children. We'd go to Starbucks to work, typing ideas for programs and lectures on the computer, and taking turns babysitting.

The truth is that when an idea is good, it will be difficult for people not to fall in love with it. Ever since I met Dennis Kennedy I knew he was, and still is, a visionary. Instantly we took roles. He is the heart of the organization and I am the muscle that moves things.

One of the first people I met was Cecilia Orellana-Rojas, a Chilean who at that time worked in the Corporate Diversity and Inclusion team for the telecommunications giant, AT&T. We went to make a presentation to her company. At that meeting I had to speak, and before making a presentation, I'd always apologized for my accent. At the end of the presentation, Cecilia got up and came straight to where I was, near the stage. She said, "You should never apologize for your accent. And you should never apologize for who you are. Because your accent is who you are." With those words she made me understand that by apologizing I was the one who was positioning myself in a lesser position, losing my opportunity before getting it.

Before long, she told us that her company could not sponsor us but that she personally wanted to support us. From this meeting, a friendship of many years was born. Cecilia was the first president of the Advisory Board in San Antonio and when she left AT&T, a decade after our first meeting, she joined us as Vice President of Strategy and Research at the National Diversity Council.

But going back to the beginnings of what today is an organization of tremendous importance and weight.

In the beginning we both worked in San Antonio, but later on Dennis moved to Houston. He was in charge of Houston and

Dallas, and I was in charge of San Antonio and Austin. That's how we started. A year later, the councils were organized.

During those first months, I did have many disagreements with my husband, Tony, because I was not making money as before. He still had his job, earned a regular salary. I told him that I had always supported him, and I asked him to support me with this endeavor. I explained to him that what he was doing, and therefore his solidarity, was not only for my benefit but the whole family.

We would work very hard, Dennis and I, to convince organizations and corporations to join our cause and sponsor us. After, we would just pray and pray to God, Mary, the saints, and especially, our Lady of Guadalupe, for a nice and juicy check to arrive. Whenever we had a miracle turned into actual money in the bank, Dennis would take a portion for our operations and then he would call me and tell me it was my turn to get a check as well.

That's how we worked the first year to make the organization a reality.

It was then that I was able to prove a hypothesis that I would have preferred not to be true. I could see that almost every time Dennis had a meeting with influential African Americans, with positions of authority in organizations, the conversation went like this: Dennis made the presentation, and the answer was, "Yes, my brother, how can we help you?" In stark contrast, when I did a presentation to Latino organizations, the answer was always the opposite, they did not see the reason why they should help. We never got the support we were looking for. I was exposed to an incredibly sad reality: as Latinos we want to believe that we support each other, that we help each other in everything, that we are very united, when reality is completely different. We come to this country with the cultural baggage of thinking that there's never enough to go around for all of us. Latinos have an embedded scarcity mentality that leads to be jealous of anyone who succeeds. I've also seen native-born Latinos discriminate against immigrant Latinos. Those types of attitudes don't exist in other groups. Perhaps there is cooperation between Latino immigrants from the same country, but there is still little appreciation for professionals who immigrated legally and made it in this country. There is no recognition of those who somehow took the opportunities and advanced. It was very painful for me not having the support from my community the way that Dennis had from his. He could go to four meetings in one day and everywhere the answer was always the same, "Yes, my brother, how can we help you?" He always left his meetings with African Americans with good news. While I not only left my meetings with Latinos with mostly bad news, but I left scolded. They treated me with contempt. One point to note is that most of these organizations did not have women in leadership positions at the time; they were men's clubs, very *macho*, who did not have an attitude of service.

When I talked to *Mami* about these troubling meetings I could see the sadness in her face. One day she said to me, "Remember what the old adage says: 'The sun rises for everyone, every day.'"

As always, her words got me thinking.

I concluded that for me that means that the opportunity exists for everyone, that there is enough for everyone. Envy and selfishness are extraordinarily strong things in our community, but we need to understand that there is an anxiety regarding not being able to have what one needs to survive. That makes us want to monopolize everything we can at that moment, which is many times more than we need. It is important to put this out there, so that we can all be aware of our shortcomings.

As immigrants we leave our countries of origin. At that moment our compatriots see us as traitors. We left and abandoned them, we no longer belong there. And in the United States we are not accepted either because we were not born here. We are nobody in nobody's land. It's happened to me. It's strange. But what's stranger is that to fit in our Latino community it's important to have a dramatic backstory (like crossing illegally or being poor before coming to the US). It seems that going through those type of hardships, and not others, like making it professionally, is the only way to be considered deserving.

It was very frustrating, disappointing, and painful to understand the dynamics of our community in the United States. And to this date I still see it.

We will never be taken seriously, even as the largest minority at sixty-two million Latinos in this country, if we do not agree, if we do not speak with one voice, if we do not support each other, if we do not join forces. We are so divided that we are our worst enemies.

If we carry this limitation in our suitcases, if we come from our countries like that, we have to break the cycle, by educating our children so that they are not like us in that sense. Educate them to know that they can only be strong and powerful when united.

I have taught my children that every time someone excels, wins an award, or has an achievement, it is important to congratulate them. Especially if it is someone from our Latino community. If one moves forward, we all move forward.

We must model good behavior when we see it. It is important to recognize the achievements of others. I surround myself with successful people because I feel the desire to achieve. I saw that in my family. We must nurture friendships with people who are better than us, so that they help us grow. We have to say what we see and what we feel and always try to get out of that circle of crushing others in order to climb. The well-known story of the frogs explains it better: When a bunch of little frogs are placed in a bucket, and become desperate trying to escape, instead of making a ladder together with their own bodies, they jump over each other pushing any of them reaching a higher spot down. As a result, none of them can make it out. We are the same, we waste too much time fighting over the crumbs among ourselves. Of course, this is an extremely sensitive issue, which is why it is easier for me to have those conversations with the new generations. They are more receptive and open to diversity and inclusion as a way of life.

Pan De Natas

1/2 Kilo de harina
50 grs. de pasas
4 huevos
azúcar al gusto
2 cucharadas de manteca
3 cucharadas de mantequilla
1 taza grande de natas
1/2 l. de leche
4 cucharaditas de royal

Modo De Hacerse

Se baten muy bien las natas enseguida la mantequilla después la manteca y bien batido se agrega el azúcar al gusto se sigue batiendo agregando 4 huevos enteros y 2 yemas y mezclado todo se pone la harina revuelta con el

To Know Ourselves Intimately, We Must Figure Out Our Weak Spots

"Flexibility is needed in order to become a successful immigrant."

I see myself as a bold, determined, loyal, and persevering woman. All of these are excellent qualities for a leader. But nobody is ever only defined by their virtues. To be able to balance our weaknesses with our strengths, we need to intimately know our vulnerable spots.

While our strengths speak by themselves, it's on our vulnerabilities that we need to work on constantly.

I have two vulnerabilities.

The first one is that I never learned how to properly fight. I can't have a difficult conversation without it affecting me to the point of feeling awful. This lack of assertiveness when it comes to speaking up, holding tight to my beliefs, and fighting for what I think is right is considered a terrible weakness or defect in the United States. It all stems from my growing up in an environment that perpetuated women as second-class citizens. I grew up hearing that a woman never raises her voice, a woman does not fight, a woman never disparages others, a woman cannot be aggressive when she's communicating. Our parents and teachers do not teach us how to speak up for ourselves. Instead, they tell us, "Your work speaks for itself." They advise us, "Don't ask for more than you deserve." They whisper to us every day, "Keep your head down when someone important speaks to you." This is our daily bread, and in our countries of origin we eat it without question. So, when we arrive in this country and are told to be assertive, to look for ways to stand out and make ourselves known, play our own drums if necessary, we find that doing so is going against our own nature, against the programming of our society, and divergent to what we've learned from people we admire.

And we question everything… Were those people we love with all our being wrong? No way. We simply need to learn to play the game by following the rules of the place where we are now living and working. Always remember: We need to be flexible to become successful immigrants.

My second weakness are my three children. Being a mom that is hands-on and always present is important to me. That is why it was difficult to have a career that required so much traveling. And yet, I have always been part of their lives, always looking for ways for us to be together and take advantage of our time as a family. I suffered a lot when they were kids, it was very painful to leave them, but I know from seeing them today that I did a good job.

And now I tell them, "I hope you know that I did the best I could with what I had. I don't know if it was enough, but I gave you guys two hundred percent." Although recently one of my sons told me, "*Mami*, you weren't always there." And I felt so bad! Dagger to the heart, my son. He didn't say it to hurt me, he was just stating a fact as he saw it. Even today I see that for Latina moms it is so difficult to handle those deep feelings of guilt, and the fear of messing up their kids when they take on more responsibilities.

I remember when I decided to leave the corporation where I worked to launch the Texas Diversity Council, the person who was there telling me, *"Tú puedes"*, "You have to do it" was my mom. I was so afraid of leaving a good position, a good job. I felt incredibly responsible for the wellbeing of my children. I'd say to *Mami*, "But what about the children?" And she'd answered me, "It's because of them that you have to do it." I didn't comprehend the truth in her words until later, when I saw that my work with the Texas Diversity Council, and later with the National Diversity Council, has not only helped others, but directly benefited my children. Yes, I had to travel a lot and had to be away often when we first started, but at the same time I worked from home. I traveled half the time, but I was also home half the time.

At our National Conference with former United States President, 2009-2017, Barack Obama. Also in the picture, members of the National Diversity Council leadership team: Jason DeGroot, Sofia Reed and Cecilia Orellana-Rojas.

With Colin Powell, former Secretary of State (2001 to 2005), retired four-star general and diplomat.

33 "Papas Rellenas al Horno"

Ingredientes

½ Kilo de papas tamaño regular
1 lata de Jamón Endiablado
50 grs. mantequilla
¼ de crema

Manera de Hacerse

Las papas se cuecen se limpian y con el cuchillo se les corta una capita se ahuecan con mucho cuidado se rellenan con el jamón se tapan con la ruedita que le han quitado se les hace unos piquetitos con el tenedor o el cuchillo y se bañan con la mantequilla derretida se les pone una cucharada de crema encima y se llevan a horno de calor regular a que doren un poquito y se sirven con más crema batida con sal.

The Audacity of Starting From Scratch

"The day you find your place in this world, you'll also find your voice."

I'm sure many will wonder: *How do you go from such a great salary to not earning anything?* The truth is that when I left JP Morgan Chase it was not just about giving up the stability of the check with several zeros and the high-level title that made me smile every time I said it out loud. No. I was saying goodbye to an important part of my life. I felt incredible sadness when I realized I had to walk away from a corporation that had given me so much, that had supported me so much, that had invested so much in my professional development, in my progress as an executive, in my improvement as a leader with a specialization in diversity and inclusion, and that offered me the opportunity to continue rising up the ranks. My heart was broken. It was the hardest thing to tell them that after everything they've done for me, I was departing.

First thing my colleagues assumed was that I had found a better job at a higher level. They couldn't believe me when I tried to explain that I was actually giving up everything in order to launch a nonprofit I didn't know would work, and that I was willing to do it without the safety of a monthly check.

They just couldn't fathom me starting a new career under those conditions.

The truth was that I was determined to accomplish every goal Dennis had set up for our new organization. Deep down I felt this was an actual calling and that if we did it right, I'd had the opportunity to bring the message of diversity and inclusion to many more people and organizations; and that way, have much more influence than what I currently had in my position with JP Morgan Chase.

My soul and my heart were thrilled. My mind, not so much. It was a daily fight within me.

My hair began to fall out of stress and fear. I knew that if this didn't work out, I had not only truncated my career at JP Morgan Chase (although I left the door open for a potential comeback, I knew that trying to do so would be a difficult task), but also left a position at a level of vice president in a multinational and multimillion dollar organization, with many benefits, an office in Manhattan, and trips that took me to wonderful places, for a position as a director in an organization that did not exist, and without salary. I placed everything aside to follow the dream of this man who came into my life unexpectedly. I didn't know it at the time, but he would become the most valuable person that ever crashed onto my life.

Every time I asked Dennis for money and tried to explain that I was the main breadwinner in our household, he'd simply replied, "Ángeles, you eat what you kill." Mainly he was conveying to me that the more organizations I visited and explained our dream to the point that they'd provide us with a donation, the better it would be for me, since I'd get a percentage of that revenue.

I was very afraid of not being able to achieve what he asked of me, but I was more afraid of failing.

Most of us have daydreamed of quitting our jobs and becoming a successful entrepreneur, but those who actually did it felt a lot of initial fear of being wrong because at that moment all they hear in their mind is: *Now I really have to prove that I can.*

In those moments of doubt, it was a such a relief to hear my mother's reassuring words. Even though we talked every day, I never told her how bad things were, but she knew that we were starting from scratch with this project and that it was just Dennis and me.

It was the beginning of the millennium and of that season that for women is so, so serious: our thirties.

Thirties for me were the years when I lived through many failures but also a great deal of achievements. When we try our best every day, we'll go through many failed attempts, but we'll also be able to celebrate successes. To me, the first was taking this giant step of saying goodbye to the corporate world and joining the world of nonprofits.

The thirties for me were also years of great growth and the beginning of this large movement for diversity and inclusion that in this country did not exist within corporations as a whole.

I entered a period of complete (re)creation. In less than a year I became what my mother was: a businesswoman. I became that businesswoman! I made my appointments, I met with the executives, I found a way to convince them that this was something they had to do for the good of their organization. At that time, we were achieving all these milestones thinking that our mission was circumscribed to Texas. The creation of the Texas Diversity Council was, at that time, our top goal.

Dennis had an idea and a vision for what he wanted for the organization. Dennis was the visionary. But he was not the practical person who was going to put theory into practice. That was me. I was the one with the experience, the one with deep knowledge of the subject, the one who had put programs into operation. My role was to support him in making his concept a reality.

The Texas Diversity Council was born in San Antonio, and it is from that first council that little by little other councils outside of Texas were created. After some time, they all were combined into what is now the National Diversity Council. When I talk to others about the origins of our organization, they are incredibly surprised that it was born in Texas, such a conservative state. My answer is that we never know where things are going to happen and how they are going to happen. Sometimes things grow where they are needed most, and ours was one of those states that really needed this infusion of ideas, of information about the value of diversity and inclusion for a company, which is not something that simply should be done because it makes those involved feel good but because it makes sense for the company, especially in a place like Texas where there is so much diversity but truly little inclusion.

Between the two of us, in less than a year we had managed to take our programs to the main cities in the state, including San Antonio, Austin, Dallas and Houston. That first year I also proposed to Dennis and launched the most successful program that we have to date, which is the Women in Leadership program.

Our first conference took place in San Antonio. To achieve this, we had to knock on many doors. One of my mentors from JP Morgan Chase participated in one of the first panels we had within this program.

Mami taught me to understand the meaning of the phrase, "Tell me who you surround yourself with, and I'll tell you who you are." And with Dennis I was able to experience it in person. There are people who can see something before anyone else does. Dennis is like that. From the start, he knew his dream was going to become true. Witnessing how he was able to bring to life what he saw so clearly in his mind was a great life lesson for me. Being by his side, being his right hand during this time of putting into practice what until then was only a theory was one of the greatest gifts. He is a man of incredible faith, he is a man who takes his Christian values wherever he goes, so he knew that this vision of his would be carried out. And that it would come about through my effort. It took me a long time to believe that this would happen. If it weren't that he saw in me that I would be the person who was going to get to the top of the mountain with him, maybe it wouldn't have happened.

It's interesting to note that he never told me why he chose me. His leadership style does not include much feedback in terms of words or emotional speeches. But he has a way of letting me know he's happy with my work.

Nevertheless, I've learned many life lessons from him. One of the most important to me is that there comes a time in our lives when we have to close our eyes, take that leap of faith and say, "I can do this. I will do this. It will be done." We must do it without considering consequences; because if we do, it'll be impossible not to realize that there's a big chance of failing… and when we see in our minds that potential outcome, we'll not even try.

Here's an example. One day Dennis told me, "We are going to do a conference on diversity and leadership. It will be the first conference in Texas where we are going to bring together all the leaders of the state committed to diversity, but we are also going to incorporate all those organizations that do not have any program that is effectively giving them the desired results or that is creating opportunities. I replied that I did not understand how we were going to do that if we did not have so many companies that were active members of the council. Without listening to me he replied, "You know what? I'm going to go rent a hotel and put it on my American Express. And it will all work out." Soon after, he returned with a signed contract with a wonderful hotel in downtown San Antonio. The approximate cost was between fifteen and twenty thousand dollars. And instead of getting dramatic about the commitment we now had to pay that amount, all he told me was that it was time to write a plan to see who the guest speakers should be, who should we try to get as panelists, who were we going to invite... After that, I had no choice but to make his proposal work.

Interesting enough, not only was the conference a raving success but we were able to raise enough funds to cover our costs and pay myself. On top of that, thanks to that event we met many individuals who became our best allies. All and all, this was the exact moment when we knew for sure that there was plenty of interest in supporting us and our concept.

Of course, in the beginning there were always those who told us we were going too big too fast. They'd encourage us to do mixers and other smaller get-togethers. But Dennis is the type of person that wants to go huge on anything. That's how he envisions things in his mind. It's my job to negotiate with him to get to an agreement that'll be satisfying yet realistic. It was easy to realize that our leadership styles and even our personalities are different, almost opposite. Dennis is an introvert who prefers to observe and analyze. However, he's funny and loves to do pranks. But most people don't get to see that side of him. I'm the other side of the coin: extrovert, social, talkative, passionate.

This conference is quite large now-a-days. In 2019 we had a record attendance, with four thousand people who came to listen former President Barack Obama. We met him in person, he congratulated Dennis and me and our entire team for the work done, he even told us that he had been watching us from afar.

Now I understand that everything is a matter of taking risks, not being afraid (and if something makes us afraid, make sure we can handle it) and getting things done. From the beginning we have always worked positively, and we have convinced ourselves that it is possible to do everything we set out to do. By modeling how to do it, by taking obstacles as opportunities and every experience as learning, we are living everything we preach and showing our community that he who believes in himself triumphs.

Our first conference was also unbelievably valuable as a measure of what we could do in the future, who we could bring as speakers and panelists, for example, which in turn weighs a lot when you are trying to attract the right people: the ones who need to hear the message, those who seek to make connections, those who need guidance. It was also important to know if our vision would work and if we could pay the debt that we had at that time.

I confess that I was in complete panic mode. In the weeks leading up to the conference, I told Dennis, "This is getting too big... all the marketing still needs to be done... this is getting to be too massive for a first event when no one knows who we are." I was throwing out there all the excuses I could find. He told me, "Ángeles, you have to believe. You have to understand that we are calling them, and they will come." Which meant that if we were making the call correctly, we had to believe that those invited would come. Frantic, I kept insisting, "But who? Who is coming?" He always listened to my concerns, but never flinched or changed his position, he remained firm in his belief that everything would work out as he planned it. That taught me to have more faith in myself and to be less concerned about the obstacles, to open myself more to the possibility of what could be achieved. It makes me think of that phrase by Rumi, *"What you seek is seeking you."*

Even though there appeared to be many reasons why the conference would fail, Dennis was right, and everything turned out exactly as he envisioned it. Five hundred people participated in that first event. Not only did we get the money to pay those expenses that scared me so much, but we also had enough to pay our wages for a while. At that moment I learned that I had inherited my mother's entrepreneurial spirit of negotiating and leading with charisma and faith. I found many who supported me because I used facts to convince them of the benefits and the impact of being on the right side of history. I understood that to obtain incredible things we must sacrifice, and often we need to change what we think about ourselves and let ourselves grow.

Mami used to tell me all the time, "The day you find your place, you will find your voice." I did not understand what she meant. She did not get to see everything Dennis and I achieved, but she was absolutely right: when I found my place, when I found my passion, when I found this career that has filled me with so much satisfaction (and also brought disappointments, and disagreements), I found my purpose in life, I found my voice. I knew then that she was right, that in this job I could always be myself, regardless of what I'm facing, and that I could always continue learning and growing.

It was also in my thirties that I learned how to be honest with myself. I gave myself permission to tell myself, *It's okay that I took this job without a salary and with so many potential negative consequences for my family. It's okay that I took a risk. I give myself permission to remain perseverant in this path. I give myself permission to stay strong and determined. I know that if I somehow fail, I'll be able to find a way to bounce back.* It may take our whole being and much life experience to give ourselves permission to fail. However, as an individual and a leader I know we can all get there.

Dennis is not afraid of rejection. I once asked him why he didn't feel sad when being rejected and he replied that because he's an African American man he has been rejected all his life. Dennis said that he'd been forsaken and looked down his entire life, and that he's heard the word "No" too many times to count… but he knew he was on the right track with the Texas Diversity Council, and nothing was going to stop him. He was already convinced that this was his dream, this was his vision, this was his purpose in life. And the most important thing, which I now acknowledge (and give myself permission to acknowledge), is that he had the conviction of saying something of extreme importance through his actions. It turns out that when he chose the person who would help him and be by his side to make it happen, and chose me —a Latina, a woman, an immigrant with an accent—, instead of someone from his African American community, he sent a message, maybe even a subliminal message, about how an African American and a Latina working and sharing together, role modeling what they preached, were truly the best advocates for diversity and inclusion, especially for those companies that did not have diversity and inclusion programs. Seeing how well we worked as a team, positively changed people's perceptions about what we presented them and how diversity and inclusion should also be a part of their core values.

He changed me and I him. Together we were able to achieve many things that would've been impossible on our own. We never thought that our top accomplishment, the Texas Diversity Council, would take us as far as it has.

Dennis Kennedy became the unexpected ingredient in my life. The ingredient I had no clue I was missing, the one I never knew was coming to change everything.

When he came into my life, he turned everything upside down.

At first I thought he was crazy and that I was even crazier to follow him.

Leaving everything behind to follow Dennis caused huge problems in my marriage. My husband would say that Dennis was truly mad and that he didn't understand why I would go along with it. I'd reply, "I know he has the best of intentions. And I know he can see something I may not see but can feel is there."

Dennis was the unexpected ingredient who helped me find the courage to see what he already saw: that I would be able to achieve and succeed in bringing to life his vision. He helped me conquer my fears and encouraged me the same way *Mami* would do when she said, "You have to somehow see in your mind's eye everything that will come to pass. And I know this organization, and all that it'll accomplish, will become a reality. I know you two will succeed."

In that first year I had to have a lot of flexibility. Think about it: I had just left a high-ranking job, the greatest achievement in my career so far, and also had said goodbye to the corporate world, with all of its opportunities, support and recognition, to go to a non-profit organization where everything I did had to be justified and there was not much margin for error.

But the most compelling thing for me was the reaction of people in the early days when they asked Dennis this question, "Why a Latina?" And inside me I'd answered, *And why not a Latina?* The shared power that we both had, him as an African American man, me as a Latina, was a fusion and a union of strengths, talents, cultures and even world perceptions. Doing things together gave us a broader platform. Our concept was diversity, equity and inclusion, and by introducing ourselves together we were already modeling what we preached every day.

When I shared with my mother that so many felt slighted because Dennis gave that much power to a Latina, she'd reply, "You can't worry about what people say or insinuate. Do not listen to any of that nonsense and instead start thinking of all the people you'll help with your work, of all the people that will see themselves in you, and of all the people that will support him because you are there. Place the weight of things where they should be, not on your person but on the impact of your actions."

I'm a people pleaser. Even more back then. I felt so much responsibility as a mother, an executive, a Latina… all the labels I carried even though I didn't want them. I knew that if I failed not only did I look bad; but, because we are ambassadors of our culture, of the weight that comes with wearing all these labels, it would make everything I represented look bad.

It was difficult to deal with it. I took it very personal. My wounds were deep. One day I was leaving a meeting and I heard that a person made a terribly negative comment about my English and my accent. I came home crying. I got very emotional. I carry my name and my cultural and family heritage with great pride. When someone attacks me, they are also attacking my family, my country of origin, everything I love the most. This type of interaction happened a lot and it made me truly angry, but then I'd realized I needed to bounce back; so, I'd go and washed my eyes, reapplied my make-up, put on my heels and my suit, and again went out to find someone who would listen to me with their mind instead of their prejudices. If I didn't go out, I didn't earn anything. I became the number one worker for the Texas Diversity Council.

I also realized early on that there are two ways to get ready for a first meeting with a potential new partner. I can prepare for the possibility of leaving empty-handed. Or I can convince myself that I'll reach my goal. I always shoot for the latter. To achieve what I want, I'll research and figure out my client's motivations and their objectives, that way I'll build up my customized plan with my client in mind. From our first client, I wanted them to feel firsthand what I was able to do for their organization and how would I become an advisor to them. I could tell them how the company would benefit from incorporating a diversity program and why it was important to obtain all the benefits that we offered. It gave me the motivation to say, "Because I'm sure about the value of diversity." Most importantly, I spoke from my own experience and the success of programs that I implemented at JP Morgan Chase. I always had the confidence to talk about those programs that I knew so intimately. I projected to clients that I was a person who knew what they were talking about, because not only had I developed the programs, but I was successful in their implementation and in the achievements obtained by the company. I let them know that we could replicate equivalent programming and help our clients achieve their goals.

It did happen several times that I'd do a presentation and was turned down by the potential client, only to find out they took my ideas as their own and implemented them. It was not a problem to me, because I could see that what I proposed to them was valuable, even if they went ahead and took credit for something I created. There is no shortage of people who want to steal our ideas for their own benefit. I remember this one time I left my proposal in one of the organizations where I made my presentation and they told me that they were not interested. Well, the following week I saw that the organization had already launched my program and the person I met with was the one who did it. There is dishonesty out there, but we are human. I don't get upset, I just move on.

Most of our prospective clients were Fortune 500 and 1000 corporations that were large, recognized, global organizations. Their history was already established. That made me realize that I could not come up with a proposal without acknowledging that they were going to be at a certain point in their journey: either very advanced or having something or nothing at all. I couldn't come to those meetings with the dicey attitude that maybe, just maybe, our proposal would work. No. I had to arrive convinced of the value of our offer and prepared to assure them that following our plan would make them more innovative in terms of their diversity, equity and inclusion at a companywide level.

I was constantly asked about Return on Investment or ROI. It was, typically, their first question/objection. They'd asked, "What's the color of diversity?". And I'd reply, "Green, green as the money you'll make with this program, because this will invest in the opportunity you're not taking; be it with your products, your marketing, or even your hiring."

Whenever I met with a client or potential client, I'd give them ideas and solutions, accordingly to all the research I've done on them before our meeting. I'd tell them that if they made this or that adjustment, they would start seeing more income coming in.

Once, I went to a well-known service store and told them that they should make a translation of their credit application so that they would reach their customers who only read in Spanish, and said that the reason being that most of their clientele were building contractors who didn't speak or read English. I told them that I would return in a month and find out how much additional money they had made from implementing this strategy. It was 2.3 million dollars! They immediately wrote a check for the Texas Diversity Council. This interaction cemented my belief that we must arrive to a meeting with ample knowledge about the company and a proposal that makes sense to them. That's why I always did my preparation and research well in advance, it allowed me to tailor every proposal to my client's needs.

It was a time of great evolution for me. I felt much more comfortable about what I was doing, and the checks started coming in more often. Within a year all the councils had been established in Texas and we already had 80 organizations that were part of our movement.

During that time, I also had to navigate being a mother of young children. I knew well my priorities: my children, above all, my faith, and my work. Everything had to be interrelated so that it could be balanced. *Mami* told me all the time, "I believe in you." And I said to myself, *I believe in you*. My mom insisted that if she did it, I would be able to do it too. I never imagined that her words and actions were going to be so important to me.

    I started to make my mom's recipes for the children. I told them these were the dishes that I grew up with. It was such an amazing time because I was working from home, but at the same time I was going out to meet successful people and billionaires. I'd come back in my suit and heels and feed the kids while we'd talk about school and homework. I was giving to them the same unconditional love I received from my mother. I remember how hard it was, and there were times when I felt like a robot moving from one task to the other, but somehow I managed to keep up with all my meetings, which sometimes involved driving to different cities in the huge State of Texas, and still tend to my kiddos. That was something else! It made me realize that we women shouldn't have to kill ourselves to do everything perfectly. It's okay to ask for help. It's okay to move that in-person client meeting to phone or virtual chat. It's okay not to clean one day. So many things that in our minds have to be perfect, but today I know that this nonsense comes mainly from ourselves, since nobody is asking us to do everything, every day at every hour. Children are not interested in a clean house, they are interested in their mother having a smile for them. Why don't we figure this out until much later in life? I think that my generation of Latina immigrant mothers arrived in this country with an impressive load of things we thought we needed to achieve so as not to disappoint anyone, in this country and our country of origin. What I've learned is that moms in the US live in a different reality. One that's more reasonable and flexible. It is not so much the number of times any of us made dinner, it is not so much the number of times we went to our son's game or our daughter's recital, but the quality of the time we spent together with them, the time when we were truly present.

    My kids are grown-ups now, but the struggles continue. When my first-born left to go to college, I lost it for a minute and wondered if I did my best in teaching him what he needed to succeed on his own. I cried for a long time but then told myself I did my best to prepare him for the real world and that those lessons would stay with him.

It was a decade of growth. There were challenges but also much joy and creativity. Even as I evolved, nothing could've prepared me for what was coming next.

My sons, my recipes, the warmth of my home… have always been the calm sea where I can rest, be myself and renew my strength so I'm ready to face the daily onslaught of enormous waves in the professional world.

"Pastel De Naranja"

1 taza de harina
2 cucharaditas de royal
½ taza de azúcar
2 huevos
25 grs. de mantequilla
jugo de naranja el necesario
tantita cáscara de N. rayada

Modo De Hacerse.

Se bate muy bien la mantequilla enseguida se agrega los yemas y el azú cuando esten de punto de Cordon se agrega el jugo de la naranja y la harina cernida con el royal cuando está bien incorporado todo se ponen las claras batidas a punto de turrón se engrasan los moldes poniéndoles galleta

Cancer and Good-Bye

*"Everything that happens,
happens for a reason."*

"Cancer" is one of those words that stops any of us in our tracks. It terrifies us. It's like a dagger that plunges deep and paralyzes us. It's a death sentence that we hope never knocks on our door. We'll do whatever we can to avoid getting it. We eat healthy, we exercise, we don't smoke, we drink in moderation, we do our required annual check-ups. And when we find out that someone we know has cancer, we feel horrified, and make the sign of the cross and pray the rosary to our most trusted saint or virgin, and praise the Lord because he's keeping us and our family safe from that kind of unimaginable suffering.

Nevertheless, none of this will keep any of us from our destiny.

I was about to turn 40 and my biggest concern at that time was what would I need to do in order to achieve new goals in the decade that I was about to start. How far was I from knowing that in an instant all this would be tossed into the place were non-fulfilled dreams are buried!

Christmas Day was approaching. Some months before, and reluctantly, my parents moved to my brother's home in Laredo. That year the whole family was together in the United States! *Mami* and I were in the kitchen, we were happy, enjoying each other's company while we prepared the delicious dishes for the Christmas dinner, which was so important in our household. We already had the dough for the *buñuelos* ready and, after letting it rest, we got ready to make the *tamales*. It was my favorite time of the year, we did everything exactly the same as when we celebrated in San Luis Potosí: first dinner, then *Misa de Gallo* at midnight and then opening gifts. The difference was that our family now had the blessing of grandchildren and of being much better off financially.

A children's choir sang Christmas carols on the radio, one of those Texas sunsets with stunning colors started to make way to the nightfall, *Mami* watched the nature's show in silence while the two of us stuffed the *tamale* dough into the leaves. It seemed a bit strange to me that she was silent. She, who was always happy, singing-talking-dancing at the same time, with so much delight that in the end she made us all joyfully dance.

I began to lose myself in my own thoughts, reviewing my calculated list of goals from forty to fifty years of age. The first one was to be the CEO of an important organization; then, to put my finances in order and on automatic pilot; I looked forward to taking my mom on an amazing trip and to do my PhD. I wanted so many things in the next decade!

In that moment I felt everything was in flawless harmony in my world and it was the perfect decade to add new and exciting achievements. Just as I was truly enjoying life, mom turned around and said those words that no child wants to hear, "I have cancer." She said it in such a soft, non-dramatic or hysterical way that at first I thought she was playing a bad joke on me, I couldn't believe I heard what I heard. Then I knew it in my heart. Without losing hope, I asked her how advanced the cancer was. I remember that sad but loving look in her eyes when she told me, "I have six months left with you, *Negrita*." I looked at her and said, "What do you mean six months?" She replied, "That's what they told me. But in those six months so much can happen. There may be a miracle. They may have been wrong in their diagnosis!"

I knew right then that that Christmas would be very special because it would be the last one we would spend together.

A haze of agonizing pain shrouded me, but I did not allow it to stay within me. I had to learn to overcome, to suppress my emotions so that they did not prevent me from doing what I had to do. I decided that I would have to be some kind of super woman and multitask as much as I could to take care of my work and my children during the week so I could travel to Laredo and be with *Mami* every weekend, and whenever else needed, for her doctor's appointments and chemotherapy treatments. Fortunately, I had the possibility of leaving Tony and Diego, who were still very young, with their father on Saturdays and Sundays, so I could focus on being with mom as much as possible.

When I took mom to her first chemotherapy treatment, she gave me the most important leadership lesson of my life. The moment she sat down on the huge medical reclining chair to receive the first chemotherapy infusion, I sat next to her, then *Mami* took me by the hand and said, "Don't be afraid. The way I prepare for this is to think that what they are putting into my body is the blood of Christ." I kept screaming inside me, *They are putting poison in your body. It cannot be something sacred. You cannot be at peace with everything that's happening. How is it possible that someone like you, who has lived a life so committed to her Catholicism, deserves this?* It was like this every single time. She never had any doubts about what she had to do, I never saw her angry about what was happening to her or what her body had to go through.

The most difficult thing in this whole process of feeling her leave me was seeing that her body began to fail her so much and understanding that she controlled the amount of suffering that she allowed us to see. *Mami* wanted to appear "normal" until the end. For example: she never stopped calling me on the phone every day, and sometimes we would talk for an hour or more. It was draining for her, but she would do it for me.

Once, I had to take her to cut her hair because it was already falling out too much. While in front of the mirror, the stylist said, "Mrs. Anita, your hair is very weak..." To which she replied, "In that case, don't worry about asking me what I want to do with my hair today. Cut it all out. There is no need to leave anything." That was the only time I saw sadness in her eyes. She turned and looked at me and said, "It's a good thing that I'm a good person, right?" I asked her why she said that. She replied, "External beauty ends for all of us. What is beautiful is what you carry within yourself. That is what remains."

Six months went by way too fast. During all that time I kept my position of responsibility with the council. Dennis would tell me, "Stop working now and go be with your mom in Laredo." He didn't understand that I had to keep busy to avoid going crazy. I was losing what I loved most in this life, which was her.

She became very weak in no time. One day she said to me, "I want to ask you a favor. I want you to take me to San Luis Potosí. I want you to take me because I am running out of time and I want to say goodbye to the city, our family, my friends. I want to go to my churches, the ones I love so much. I want to say goodbye to that place where I was so happy." I immediately said yes and told her I'd take her. She could no longer get on a plane, so we drove with my sister. It was one of the things I am most grateful for. When I told Dennis about my travel plans, he told me not to worry about anything, to just go and completely focus on her.

We were there the whole week. It was a magical journey. We laughed so much. We ate so much. We went to visit so many places. It was Easter week and San Luis Potosí has a Spanish tradition, The Procession of Silence, which takes place on Good Friday. They take all the icons, statues, and paintings out of the churches, and the city comes to a halt. It is a very solemn moment. The feeling of devotion permeates everyone there. Thousands of people participate. Because my mom was in a wheelchair and in poor health, we were given a great front row space to watch the procession go by. It was the only time in those six months that I saw her cry. She said, "There is a reason this had to happen to me, but I don't know why. And I'm scared". She was sixty-seven years old.

Her cancer got worst and metastasized shortly after we returned from México. Until then, it seemed that chemotherapy was doing something for *Mami*. But cancer is like that, it is a sneaky disease, first you believe that everything is going well and suddenly the sledgehammer falls at the least expected moment. As a last attempt, I decided to bring her to San Antonio because they told me of a specialist who could help her. At that time I did not know that this was the last week that she would be with us. We took her to a hospital and together we took turns to be with her, since we did not want her to spend even a second on her own.

One night, *Papi* stayed with her, neither of them spoke English very well and they had a very unpleasant experience with a nurse who treated *Mami* very badly, treated her so terribly that she even made her cry. I was furious. I wondered how a health worker could be so harsh with a patient who was dying. My mother realized what was happening and asked me to come over to her bed. She said, "Don't worry about this, it's not a problem for me. I want you to know something that I have not been able to tell you before, but I want to tell you now in front of your dad. I know that right now you will not understand it and maybe you will not understand it for a long time, but something exceptionally good is happening here and something very big is going to come out of all this. I don't know what it is, but I know I have to tell you." Then she fell asleep. I turned to look at my dad and said, "What good thing can happen as a result of me losing her? There is nothing positive that can happen as a result of me losing my mother."

She never got to see all that Dennis and I accomplished. She was never able to go to any of our amazing conferences. She never saw the impact of our work. I think she left thinking: *My daughter is going to do something impressive*; but she never saw it.

After losing her, I went back to work immediately. I didn't want to take time off. I felt that I had to emotionally support my children and *Papi*, who came to live with me. They were married forty-seven years. When friends asked me, "How is your dad?" I'd reply, "Daddy is no longer living after losing her, he is dying every day."

Papi passed away three years after her. He died of a heart attack. There was not a single day that he did not dedicate himself to honor the memory of *Mami*, there was not a day that he did not talk to his grandchildren about their grandmother, there was not a day that he did not miss her. In a way I think his pain was so deep that he was happy to die and go be with her again. I was going to miss him.

With his death I lost my mom and dad in three years.

At that time I didn't know that two years after that my marriage was going to end too.

I remember how much stronger my faith became at that time in my life. It was as if I wanted to hold on to something that would give me solace and even motivation to see straight and do what I needed to do to continue without my parents by my side. My boys were still young, and I realized that there was no other way but forward. I continued to live for them even when I had lost both my parents and my husband. But I had this detrimental mental conversation going on, I would say to myself, *Ángeles, it is not normal for someone to lose so many people in their life in such a short time. Something is wrong with you.* I never knew if that was true or not. That something was wrong with me. But I couldn't dwell on the negative. And I fought with the little strength I could muster to try to wake up every day, go to work, fulfill my responsibilities with my family and even be grateful for what I did have.

Just two short years later I was savagely hit again by death when my sister died due to medical negligence in a hospital where she was being treated. She left behind her son, Mario, who was 9 and I adopted. In the blink of an eye, I was a single mother with three sons.

By then the Texas Diversity Council had grown so large that we were perfectly positioned to launch the National Diversity Council, a nationwide council with representation in twenty-eight states. As a result, the workload grew, so did the number of employees needed to operate smoothly, the amount of conferences we held, and the multiple leadership programs we created and run. Everything was bigger but we never lost our focus: spread the ideas that lead to greater diversity, equity and inclusion in companies and organizations of all kinds.

I was traveling a lot, so I hired a lady to come and live with me so that the children would have someone to stay with.

It was a time of great pain personally, but of incredible achievement on the professional level.

On the family side of the scale, I was running almost on empty due to all the losses I suffered; but on the professional side of the scale, I was amazed at everything that had been achieved. Just as *Mami* predicted on her deathbed, something impressive happened, though on a level and magnitude we never imagined.

With Papi, Jesús Martínez Gamez, in San Antonio.

Pastelitos de Anita

- 1 cucharada de sal
- 4 tazas de harina
- 6 cucharadas grandes de servir de azúcar
- 2 tazas chicas de manteca
- 4 yemas
- 2 naranjas grandes
- 1 cuchara de carbonato
- 300 gramos de azúcar y canela

Modo de hacerse

En una cacerola se bate la manteca, el azúcar y las yemas y la raspa dura de las naranjas hasta que la pasta haga hojitos se pone enseguida la harina y carbonato se amasa con el agua de las naranjas hasta dejar la masa a punto de torta se cortan al gusto y se revuelcan en el azúcar y canela.

Fin

Searching for a New Balance

*"Take a risk,
state your truth, say what you want to say.
Show the door to everything that's limiting you,
tell that version of yourself to vacate your mind.
You are capable of achieving your goals."*

When well-intentioned people asked me if I was sad or depressed because I had turned 40, I wanted to scream, "I'm alive. My mother has passed away. Turning 40 is not important to me right now." When we go through huge losses and deep grief, our perspective changes. What before appeared to be crucial becomes completely irrelevant.

The loss of my mother meant I needed to search for new role models. I started to look for women that inspired me. I dusted off all my Frida Kahlo books, the ones I'd been reading since my teen years, way before it became popular in the United States. When I read her journal, it gave me solace. I knew that I was not the only one who went through what I was going through, that my feelings were not strange, that I was not alone in my sorrow.

I did go through a stage where I wanted to be left alone. Plainly, I did not want to deal with other people's emotions when they were around me. Even though I was the organization's face, I tried to stay away from the limelight. Just going through the motions of getting my picture taken felt like my grief was too exposed. I needed my time, so I stayed away as much as possible of social events and dedicated myself to my kids.

Nobody is ever ready for the passing of their parents. We know it's going to happen, but that doesn't prepare us. However, losing my sister at such a young age and in such cruel fashion was what threw me over the edge. Keeping the "I'm great" façade in business meetings and conferences took a huge emotional and physical toll. Just making it to a symposium, presenting on a specific topic, interacting with colleagues, was an accomplishment in itself. When someone would ask me, "How are you?" I'd reply, "I'm fine," and then I'd smile and give them a hug. I kept my mask on the outside, but on the inside I felt like the person in Edvard Munch's "The Scream" painting.

Little by little I calmed down. We had a lot to do, and I knew that my family, and especially *Mami*, were blessing each and every one of my steps as they looked after me from Heaven.

There was this line from a poem from Amado Nervo, one of my favorite writers, that kept coming to my mind, *"I'm the architect of my destiny."* I'd repeat those words as a mantra since I'm sure we are the ones in charge of building our lives through our actions, our decisions, our successes as well as our failures, and the way we deal with everything that shows up at the shores of our lives.

I went through immense loss as a human being and enormous growth as a leader during that period. Even as I was anxious and baffled at times, to the point of getting scared of failing, I never lost my focus or strayed from the path. I was keenly aware of what mattered and what I needed to do in order to fulfill all my responsibilities. As challenging as this period of my life was, it also brought me great personal and professional evolution.

All and all it was the perfect time to let go of my extra baggage. It was an opportunity to refine and redefine objectives and place my attention and energy on the things that needed to be taken care. Our organization was growing and had more allies, supporters, and partners. We were plotting our next steps and opening new councils in different states. My responsibilities expanded. Today I believe I was able to bounce back because all the emptiness caused by death was immediately filled with my priorities, my children, and my career. They were my responsibility and my pride at the same time. Giving to each of them exactly what they needed I found a way to go on.

The organizations that became our clients looked to me for the best advice and programming their money could buy. Efficiency and return on investment are always the ultimate goals when dealing with large corporations. It was up to me to deliver on everything we promised. If we wanted to keep going and expanding, failing them was not an option.

From our early days, the mission of the National Diversity Council has always been to become the main resource to organizations and businesses that want to implement new diversity and inclusion programs. We also wanted to become a credible source to the ones who didn't have programming or were on the fence about it.

Hard work paid off for us and we got to the goal of serving two-hundred organizations, and then three-hundred, and four hundred, and so on. We were growing so fast that I didn't have the time to go to a corner to cry and mourn. The little spare time I had went to my children. As a single mom, I felt I needed to give them two hundred percent since I played the role of mom and dad.

One of the strange things I remember from that time was how much I avoided being the face of the organization because I didn't like how emotionally exposed that made me feel; but while denying myself that role, I was also pushing down much of who I truly was, thus limiting my own potential.

I believe many Latinas go through similar scenarios when they are trying to find their own voice and their true role in life. We are culturally conditioned to wait until we are acknowledged, to try not to talk too much, to avoid being the center of attention, to be humble. We were taught that way. However, when we find ourselves in a leadership position, we need to find the courage to give up on the culturally instilled customs that hold us back. Remember: we are doing this not only for ourselves, but for everyone that we'll help by opening new doors with our actions.

Women, and specially the so-called women of color, have been so limited for so many centuries that's hard to imagine there's a better way for all of us. I confess I did waste too much of that precious time hanging on to my fears and culturally learned false meekness. By my 40s I had enough of that. I decided to leave my comfort zone and venture beyond what I'd been told were my borders. I longed to explore new opportunities and figure out for myself how far could I go.

To the tormented Ángeles that I was then, I'd say today, *"Take a risk, state your truth, say what you want to say. Show the door to everything that's limiting you, tell that version of yourself to vacate your mind. You are capable of achieving your goals."*

When my mother died, I lost my daily cheerleader, the one person that encouraged me with words of affirmation and showed me how to see the positive in everything. When she left, her voice was also silenced in my mind. I was in so much pain that I couldn't be persuaded by anyone to take new paths. I felt total apathy. I know nobody noticed it, but to me it was like the world had no color.

It was then, when I least expected it, that Dennis Kennedy offered me the position of CEO, National Diversity Council. In this occasion it was me asking, "Why me?" Dennis replied, "It has to be you because you know the work and everything we have achieved together... Even if I tried, I couldn't be able to find another person who has more passion and is more qualified than you to do this. You have already done it, you have already proven your worth in this organization, you are part of this."

Even though I surely could agree with what Dennis told me, I had my doubts about the appropriateness and the timing. So, I asked my kids for a family meeting.

When the four of us were together, I said to them, "I've been given the opportunity of becoming CEO of the National Diversity Council, but I don't want to take this decision without consulting with you. If I take this job, I'll have to give it my all, which means more time at work." They answered in unison, "Of course you have to do it, mom. They need you." I tried to explain further, "If I take it, I'll miss more games, more recitals, more of your events…" My oldest, Tony, replied, "This is what needs to be done, mom. We cannot be selfish and tell you to stay still, when we know that what you do at work has a great positive impact in the lives of so many people." I was dumbfounded. I said to myself, *Here I have my fourteen-year-old son telling me this, when all this time I have carried the guilt of having to leave them to go on my trips and my meetings ... And here I have this person telling me this, "We cannot be selfish, we have to do it."*

It's important to recognize that many women who are mothers and have a professional career they enjoy feel guilty about it. I think we can look at it from a different angle. We can rest assured that we are raising our children, boys and girls, to be true feminists who some day will do away with all of the nonsensical role descriptions we live by today. No man leaves home in the morning feeling guilty because they are going to work. I've never come across a man who would say, "I'm in pain every time I have to leave my wife and kids because of traveling for work."

Since I was a single mom, I also decided to teach my children to work with me as a team when it came to home chores. Each one had a responsibility and learned how to do everyday tasks, such as cooking, laundry, cleaning, and so on. It was great not only because it brought us even closer as a family but also because one day they will be on their own and I wanted them to be capable and independent. I imagine them when they have their wife, their home, their own family, and how nice would it be to have raised a man that is there for his spouse in every aspect of life. And being the Latina mom I am, I'd tell them, "Well I don't want to hear your partner say, 'Your mother didn't teach you to do anything.' Imagine that!"

I reflect my mother's voice and my children reflect their grandmother's voice through me. I understand now that my mother's voice never faded but became another kind of voice. We are all ingredients reinventing recipes from one generation to another. What we pass on to our children is what we will see in them. The same happens with bosses and their employees.

One very nice thing is that always, since they were very young, I have practiced my speeches with them as my audience. I remember a lot of laughter and nonsense during those preparations when they were kids. I did it to practice my English, my pronunciation, the pauses, and all that. What I never imagined was that many of the ideas, and even the phrases I would say, along with bringing them to my events and conferences, would become an important part of their education as human beings. They assimilated everything and later made it their own.

Today, I am proud of the young men they have grown into. I am not sure which one will follow in my steps. It will most likely be Diego, as he is interested in becoming an immigration attorney. I see how committed he is, very vocal in expressing his concern with the constant mistreatment of other groups. Currently, he's as concerned as I am about Asian American and Pacific Islanders, since they've had a very difficult time being blamed for the global pandemic, a narrative started by a racist administration at the height of the crisis in 2020. The violence and hate crimes endured by this community continues to escalate and of course my sons, who have learned compassion and solidarity throughout their lives, are the first to point out how much work we need to continue to do as a society and as a country to be more inclusive and broadminded. I am hopeful that the next generation will not only carry on with this important work but take it to its next levels.

*Moments of goofiness with my sons.
Because life shouldn't be serious all the time!!!*

With Dennis Kennedy and journalist Soledad O'Brien (of Australian and Cuban heritage).

With former Florida Governor and former presidential candidate, Jeb Bush, during the 2008 Diversity and Leadership Conference in Dallas, Texas. Next to him is Winell Herron, H-E-B's Group Vice president of Public Affairs, Diversity and Environmental Affairs. During that conference we also had the participation of Chaz Bono (transgender LGBTQ), Tony Plana (Cuban American) and Spike Lee (African American). This is relevant because the NDC is a non-partisan organization that seeks to always include everyone in everything we do.

RECETAS DE DULCES.

#1 PIRULINES.—
PARA 1 KILO DE AZÚCAR.

Se pone a hervir el agua con el limón, luego se le agrega el azúcar, se deja hervir hasta que espese, luego se le agrega la pintura vejetal. Para saber cuando está se pone un vaso lleno de agua y se le agrega el dulce caliente, cuando se ponga duro el dulce, está en su punto. Fin.

PIPITORIA DE AJONJOLÍ.
PARA 1 KILO DE AZÚCAR.

Se pone a hervir el azúcar con el limón, cuando ya esté en su punto se le agrega la Pintura Vejital y se derrama sobre una tabla limpia (con manteca para que no se pegue) luego que esté este tendido el dulce se le agrega el ajonjolí por encima y cuando se enfríe se corta con un cuchillo al gusto. FIN.

How to Be a Successful Leader

> *"A pitcher is nobody without his team and the support of every single one of its members."*

As of 2021, only twenty three percent of working women hold top executive positions. A miniscule four percent of this group are women of color. We are a long way from a fifty percent parity in representation. The changes have not occurred as quickly as we would like. However, a variety of studies have proven, over and over again, that when organizations have female executives at the highest levels, as well as women leading work teams, they obtain better results in all aspects of business, including ROI. The reason is simple: women are better at organizing; our minds have the ability to work on five things at the same time without losing track of any. A woman can be cooking, giving guidance to an employee, checking her son's homework, silently shouting at her other son, ordering something online... and everything works out seamlessly. Ask a man to do the same tasks at the same time and his head will explode. You have to give him a specific list! This unique ability most women possess needs to be sought out and taken into consideration by every single organization that wants to ensure they'll stay ahead of the pack and will always get best results. We know that no matter their current prestige and standing, organizations are left behind when they do not move with the times and refuse to evolve.

Six tips for being a successful leader.

Seek to nurture our positive thoughts so that we can always be mightily empowered. If we are not sure about who we are, the value of what we do, the potential we have; and of top of that, we make ourselves invisible because we are afraid of failure, we will never get out of the comfort zone. We must nurture our positive beliefs to empower ourselves. We can't wait for someone else to do it for us. Instead of being dominated by thoughts and emotions that do not serve us, we have to take control of our life. Negative thoughts like, "My English is not good," "They will not understand me," "They will laugh if I speak up..." should not have space in our minds. Everything that limits us does not serve us.

Identify our talents and abilities and learn to use them. Behind each of our achievements there's always going to be sacrifice and strength. Within our failures there are lessons. That's why it's so important we don't see them solely as failures, otherwise we will never learn from them. If we make a mistake, we should learn our lesson the first time and move on. It is important to recognize our capabilities and to use the tools that will lead us to do things that perhaps even we did not know we could achieve.

Look for inspiration in other successful women. When we open our minds and our spirits to explore the stories of other successful women, who inspire us to see that anything and everything can be done, we recognize that they overcame the barriers that were imposed on them. And when we see other women in our environment achieve their own goals, let's try not to be envious of them but rather be supportive and say, "You did really good. Tell me: How were you able to reach your goals?" Congratulate that woman and see in that person someone who has made a difference for all of us. As girls we were raised hearing that we had to be the prettiest, the most educated, the finest, the softest. Well, it shouldn't be like that anymore, we mustn't compete with each other to accomplish our own dreams.

Invest our time developing worthy relationships. To grow, we must build trusted connections in different social and work environments. When we have those kinds of relationships we can find a mentor, a sponsor, a coach. We can find women who give us good advice. If we focus only on achieving goals, but we do not develop that ability to relate, we'll find out that we can reach the goal but only on our own. Wouldn't it be easier if we surrounded ourselves with people who supports us, advises us, and encourages us?

Learn to speak up. This is an extremely important task for immigrant Latina women. This means giving ourselves permission to shine, not feeling sorry for being a star. Taking the risk to express our ideas is a must. If we don't do it, no one is going to do it for us. Each one of us has to become their fan number one. If we cultivate a positive image of ourselves, we are acknowledging that we are skilled, prepared and ready. Then we will feel more confident in demanding what is reasonable and what is fair as we share our brilliant ideas, especially in difficult times. And it is by letting our own voices out that we'll feel like we can take advice, take larger risks, and share our experiences with others.

Remember that the leader who inspires confidence in their team members receives a vote of confidence from them. My father was a baseball pitcher for a long time. He always told me, "A pitcher is nobody without his team and the support of everyone who is playing with him." This is leadership in an organization. A true leader is one that not only leaves a mark on everything, but also has trust in each member of the team and provides constant learning opportunities. And the most important thing that can exist is the trust that a team has in its leader, as well as the trust that the leader has toward its team. This is something I experience daily with my work team. In critical moments the leader must speak to the people in their team frankly, with sensitivity, with conviction, allowing themselves to be vulnerable in front of their team members by also sharing what they feel. The 2020 pandemic offers the perfect example. When we were entering a period of complete uncertainty, I was able to express that I was afraid while encouraging my team, especially since we had just closed an excellent quarter and were in an advantageous position. When we tell the truth, the team responds and acts based on that transparency and the personal history we have with them, especially if you've never lied to them. We need to make it a point to be surrounded by people who believe in us and in whom we also believe.

I accomplished one of my big dreams and became CEO of the National Diversity Council before I was fifty. I achieved that goal with the approval of the entire board of directors of the national council, which is made up of many high-ranking people in their respective companies and organizations. I was coming from being president to being CEO. But as I arrived at the highest level in the organizational ladder, I quickly realized how lonely of a place it was. I didn't change, I was the same Ángeles as always, but the people around me begin to see me in a different way. In a short time I understood who would stay with me and who would leave my life. It was very painful to see that for some people my new position was cause for consternation and envy. Maybe it felt worst because I am not like that. When I see that someone succeeds, I celebrate it because I understand it as a manifestation of that person. Also, I believe that when someone wins, I don't lose —that's a dysfunctional perspective. I never imagined that there were people who feel awful when someone other than themselves succeeds. But I experienced that scenario firsthand. I didn't want to believe it, but it's true that envy is the mother of all sins. This time it wasn't just "why her?" but also "she is not from here." Being a Latina immigrant and a woman did not, according to them, made me worthy of what I had earned through hard work, perseverance, discipline and dedication.

From my own experiences, the most envious detractors of immigrant Latinos are US-born Latinos who believe that opportunities should go solely to them. Perhaps I am to blame somehow, and that's because the little time I spent in town, when I was not traveling, was dedicated to my family. The result was that I neglected to cultivate the necessary interpersonal relationships where I would have had the opportunity to let people in San Antonio get to know me. As Latinos we fail each other by not accepting and not including ourselves. How important can it be that I was born in another country? What does it matter if I identify myself as an immigrant? What does it matter if I didn't grow up in the United States? There have been people who have said it to my face, "Ángeles, you are not from here, you did not grow up here, so you do not understand our experience." That is true, but I identify with them because I have studied their history and I recognize their struggle.

Another difference is that I am completely bilingual and that creates resentment since I can speak English without having lost the Spanish that I love so much. That is an incredible advantage, speaking multiple languages. Only in this country can the ability of speaking multiple languages not be valued. We have even gone through times when parents did not teach their children the language of their country of origin, forcing them to only speak English as a way to ensure that no one would mistreat them. I recognize the history of oppression experienced by many Mexican Americans, who, if they spoke Spanish at school, were punished, beaten and so on. Today I make it a point to invite English-only Latinos to learn Spanish, since it is their language and part of their heritage. I tell them that learning to speak Spanish benefits them.

We've been told that speaking Spanish is a "deficiency" in Latinos, and I know it's not. We are who we are, and we are proud of it. We need to change the tables, show everyone our true fighting spirit, and say, "You are wrong. I do want and can learn my language and my culture because it is an advantage for me. The real disadvantage is to accept it when they tell me that I can't."

With Cuban American actor and activist, Tony Plana. He's a great friend and an ally to the Council since our inception. He's a person who's always fighting to better the education of Latinos in the United States.

Pictured with América Ferrera, artist and activist of Honduran descent, during our National Diversity & Leadership Conference. During the presentation I decided to put the photo of both when we were children, and it was a surprise for her when she came out on stage with me. These two brunette girls, similar to the girls who are detained in centers for the undocumented on the border today, became successful immigrant women, mothers and contributors to seeking just, humane and legal solutions to the immigration crisis in the US.

Polvorones de Canela

1 kilo de harina
230 grs de azúcar
2 cucharas de carbonato
2 "   "   "   canela
6 yemas se baten con 4 cucharas
agua se agrega la canela
enseguida las yemas y luego
azúcar enseguida la harina con
carbonato se baten bien y se [hacen]
bolitas.

Fin

Galletas de Maizena

Se bate una clara y cuando esté
a punto de nieve se les pone
suficiente azúcar y canela a
gusto nueces picadas y cocoa
y maizena hasta que junte todos
los ingredientes en el punto se
hacen cucharaditas en costra

Fin

Ingredients of Success
For Immigrant Women

"On the way to success you'll find people screaming at you, trying to distract you. You have to completely silence them and focus on your goal."

As immigrants coming to this country, we must be open to the idea that not everything is going to happen as we imagine. We should acknowledge that obstacles will present themselves and problems will arise. We need to understand that everything we accomplish will cost us a lot more than US-born and raised Latinos. Understanding those facts will help us seek the inner strength needed to persevere.

I am a very analytical person. In the beginning I spent a lot of time analyzing in detail every situation that came up. As time went by, I realized that not everything is going to have a reason or a logic, but that sometimes things just happen.

These are my tips for immigrant women who dream of finding success.

Focus completely on the task at hand and do not allow distractions. One of the things that helped me the most throughout my career was a lesson my dad gave me inside the baseball diamond. I was about eight years old, and my dad took me to train with him; he wanted to teach me to throw the ball like a good pitcher. Right away I realized I wasn't particularly good at it: I couldn't throw far enough or with the needed strength. I also couldn't understand why *Papi* insisted on me learning the game since there were no female baseball players back then. I kept thinking that he was insisting on something that wouldn't work for me, that he was wasting his time with me.

After a long time throwing and hitting the ball without rest, I felt very tired, my arm hurt, and I started asking my father if we could be done already with practice. Seeing me so flustered, he took pity on me. He walked to me, knelt in front of me and while lifting the baseball he said, "This is a life lesson. Going out in the world you'll find that life is similar to this game. You will never know what is going to come to you, from where and how fast. The most important thing you must learn from this is to always keep your focus and not let anything stop you from reaching your goal."

It was a valuable lesson that I brought with me to the United States as an immigrant. Distractions come disguised in many ways. They come concealed as friends and foes, as loud opinions, as media and strangers who tell us to return to our country of origin because we do not belong there. Learning to focus on that goal, hitting that precise center he talked to me about, meant being able to remove all that doubt, all those voices, all those distractions that were disguised in many ways and that limit us as immigrants because they are always present in our life, trying to trip us up.

I asked him what being focused meant to him. *Papi* replied, "When we played, there were always people yelling about everything. I had to block them from my mind, focus on my movements, not listen to anyone, and put my attention on throwing the ball so that it hit precisely in the center of the catcher's glove." His words were always with me, especially when I felt that someone or something was trying to steal my attention with distractions, noise, and hateful words. Every time a "little monster" appeared trying to make me lose concentration, I remembered dad's words and immediately silenced everything and everyone that could annoy me, make me fall, or prevent me from hitting the center. It was the only way to move to my next objective as if nothing bothered me. I was not going to let anyone take my focus off the goal or move me from the line that showed me the way to the door I wanted to open. I think that every immigrant must persevere using this technique so they can reach their goals.

To define our target, we must be honest with ourselves. When we take a decision, we must be prepared to deal with the consequences, whatever they may be. Therefore, the decision must be the right one for each of us. I make decisions trying to see the whole game: this is my action plan, these are my goals, this is the final objective; so, what are my options and how am I going to get where I want to go? We will always find obstacles, whether in a corporate career, or when we arrive in this country... Many think that being in the United States is the ultimate goal. It's not. Our final target is still far away, and our new path has only just begun. Immigrants start from a little further away than the others, we start with "perceived deficiencies." Being Latino and immigrant likely classifies us as less, it automatically affixes on to us unfair labels, prejudices and stereotypes. Even those who are professional come to realize that their degrees and experience from their countries of origin tend to be perceived as of inferior quality and value as those acquired in the US. And yet, when someone underestimated me, I would just smile and tell myself that they would soon see what I was really made of. And whenever I achieved my goals, I saw that they couldn't understand how I got to where I wanted and they'd whispered, "And how did this one accomplish that?" "How did she achieve that?" "How did she learn?" "How...?" The answer is that I did not waste time with distractions and that while they were busy underestimating me, I kept moving forward.

Changing plans is a normal component of the immigration experience. If we took a survey of immigrants in this country, we would see that a large percentage of us are doing something different today than what we thought we were going to do when we were in our countries of origin. We must adapt to what is available and open our eyes to new opportunities. As immigrants, most of us are not only going to make it happen, but we are going to excel. And if it means that we must leave our comfort zone, be it professional or personal, we are going to do it. Why? Because at the end of the day, when we see that we must provide for ourselves and our families, pride goes out the window and we will look for ways to survive, to support the family that we have uprooted from their country of origin. That may mean that if any of us were an engineer, lawyer, doctor, journalist, or any other professional before arriving in the United States, it is likely we'll have to let go and do something different. So be it! We are in for the long game. For me there is nothing wrong or shameful in having to start from scratch. Furthermore, I am not ashamed to say where I come from and how poor we were, not at all, it is a validation of the human spirit to be able to tell others about my circumstances before coming here, how I got to where I am and that I plan to continue climbing and excelling. "A rose grows in the midst of so many thorns," my mom used to say. That's how we immigrants are, we don't give up no matter the obstacle. That's why changing plans is not only normal, but when we accept those shifts wholeheartedly, we open ourselves to finding new routes, new experiences, new opportunities. Take me, for example, I went from engineering to human resources, the game changed me completely, I adapted, and, in the end, it turned out that my new career, which I never thought I would find, was what I really wanted.

The types of opportunities immigrants come upon in the United States cannot be found in their own countries of origin. It is a shame it works that way. And I say it, not because I do not love my country of origin, quite the opposite, the further away I am from México the more I love it, but that does not mean that I am blind to the things that forced me to seek the opportunity elsewhere and to the responsibility that our governments have to build the necessary environment so that talented people do not feel like they have to leave in order to achieve. Politics aside, it is liberating that upon arriving at the US we can choose the path we want and that at the end of the day the only (major) obstacle is typically ourselves.

To give ourselves equal opportunities, we should learn English. The immigrant who has the desire to learn the language used in the professional and business world, English, will learn it. But whoever decides to put up a fight or be openly reluctant, will not learn it. Each of us needs to adapt to the way things are done here. Learning English does not mean losing Spanish, on the contrary, we can give ourselves more opportunities by embracing bilingualism and multiculturalism. From the beginning it was clear to me that I needed to learn English to be able to communicate but that I would never give up my Spanish.

An interesting point to think about is how each of us define success...

Success for me is defined as the happiness of being at peace with the person that I am. It is sleeping comfortably every night and waking up every day and being able to feel the joy that I exist, that I am me, that I manifest myself, that I am in harmony with the world. It is not easy to get to that place of light. That is why happiness and success are synonymous for me: being able to be happy with the person I've become, looking with joy at everything I've done in my life and the impact my actions have had on the lives of others.

I see life from the perspective of tranquility with myself. If I had to choose between success, as most define it, and happiness, I would choose happiness. I have not always had a high position and an outstanding salary, and I have been happy; and when I have had it, I have also been happy. In my life I have been able to observe that many people who have money and material things are not happy. It is practical to have it, but it does not promise happiness. I come from having nothing and I am not afraid of going back to that. Money and power have not corrupted me. My "perceived image" does not define me as a person, it reflects on the organization I lead but not on me. I am still the same Ángeles who welcomes opportunities with open arms, the one who humbly seeks to benefit others with her actions. Peace and a true smile are the most important to me.

12 ## Polvorones De Naranja
¼ k. de harina
150 grs. de manteca
media cucharita de carbonato
1 naranja
2 huevos
3 cucharadas de azúcar

Modo De Hacerse
Se bate la manteca con el azúcar hasta que esponje enseguida se agregan 2 yemas después el carbonato cernido con el harina raspar un poco la naranja poniendole el sumo de la misma se revuelve con la punta de los dedos si queda seca se agregan las claras batidas a punto de turrón esta pasta debe quedar propia al extenderse que sea de ½ cm. de grueso

The Art of Transforming Problems Into Solutions

"From this tragedy something extraordinary will be born."

The words that *Mami* said to me when she had little time left to live, stating that something good would come out of everything that was happening to her, were for me bitter to swallow. I was so shocked. The pain of losing her hit me ruthlessly and stunned me so badly that I couldn't understand what she wanted to say to me. It took me a long time to grasp the depth of her message; but when I did, I realized that we all have the power to turn something bad that has happened to us into something beneficial and even transformative.

Because of her lack of English, my mom was treated by healthcare personnel with racism and disrespect at a vulnerable stage in her life. It made her feel so awful that she wanted to leave the hospital. I could see that *Mami* was not the only one, that the same thing was happening to many of the foreign and immigrant patients hospitalized there.

After she left us, I would dream of her already at death's door, emaciated, without her hair. A short time later, I had a dream in which I saw her as she was before cancer: pretty, cheerful, happy, jovial... And she was telling me something. As soon as I woke up, I realized that making a reality her last words, "Something good has to come out of this tragedy," was in my hands. That very same day I started to work in what today we know as the Healthcare Diversity Council.

When the worst of my grief came to an end, I was able to realize that what ailed our healthcare system in the United States was lack of cultural competence amongst their staff at all levels. I made a list of things that needed to be addressed and contacted doctors and hospitals to float my proposal. Basically, I wanted to ensure that hospital staff had interpreting services available, and that they were able to take measure of their patients' cultural backgrounds and their views of western medicine, even taking into consideration the healing methods and natural remedies they are more accustomed to use. I also spoke with my contacts in the field about access to healthcare and inequities regarding the treatment of minorities.

It was a program so well received that its first sponsor was MD Anderson Cancer Center in Houston, Texas.

The passing of Obamacare, or the Affordable Care Act, as well as the Covid-19 global pandemic were events that brought the topics I cared for to the front of the conversations regarding healthcare. Those events made it crystal clear that many of our hospitals are not ready to efficiently serve minorities, immigrants, and foreign populations.

Let's take, for example, immigrants and Latinos, by far the largest and fastest growing minority communities in the United States. This is important because it is those groups that face the most challenges when seeking health care and medical attention.

I spent six months in different hospitals while *Mami* was in treatment. At that time, I observed that within all the ethnic minorities, it is Latinos that have the hardest time accessing health insurance. This is especially true for Latino immigrants, regardless of their immigration status. African Americans follow as the second largest uninsured group, when compared with their White counterparts.

There are many barriers to accessing health insurance coverage and protection. For example, *Mami*, who was in the country legally, did not qualify for any kind of help in the hospitals where we went. This was before the Affordable Care Act.

When my mother told me in her last days of life that "something good is going to come out of this tragedy," she was giving me permission to take the essence of her suffering to people with influence. She was telling me that what was happening to her in that moment was also happening to millions across the country. It was as if she had said to me, "You have the opportunity and the possibility to make this visible. Make them realize what is happening."

While I was taking care of my mom at the hospital I met and got to know other families who were walking the same path as us. So many patients and their families, who did not spoke English or were not fluent, going through such a difficult time made even harder because of communication and cultural barriers. Understanding what the doctor and their team are trying to convey is a matter of life or death. Even when working with an interpreter, it's necessary to find the right words and make the message as true to the original as possible. If the interpreter does not recognize or incorrectly translates specific words, there may be problems as a result. The different types of Spanish and the hundreds of indigenous languages in Latin America are filled with variations and nuances only well-trained and experienced professionals are capable of detecting and correctly addressing. However, access to qualified interpreters who are culturally competent is a major problem in many communities.

Using the Latino community as an example, let's talk about the most common challenges to access healthcare services.

1. Socio-economic challenges: A higher percentage of Latinos live in poverty, which tends to mean less access to education, high unemployment rates, working in fields where it is less feasible to be offered health insurance (as is the case in construction, agriculture, services, or manufacturing, to name a few.)

2. Cost of health insurance: It is impossible for a family that earns minimum wages to pay for insurance that costs a large percentage of their income. And in the case of being able to access cheaper insurance, the problem is that coverage is limited.

3. Shortened workweek: Nowadays it is common that workers are offered jobs that come below forty hours a week, thus not offering health insurance. There are also the jobs that offer medical insurance after a "trial period" that may extend to several months.

4. The patient's immigration status: Undocumented immigrants face the greatest obstacles in terms of health services and health insurance. They are excluded from receiving any type of federal aid when purchasing health insurance. In 2020, even with some access to the Affordable Care Act, about seven million undocumented immigrants were unable to get any form of health insurance. We also see that a high percentage of immigrants with legal status, including permanent residents and naturalized citizens, lack basic health insurance.

5. Exclusion: The lack of knowledge of available services, the high cost of health services, and the lack of culturally and linguistically competent medical services lead to the exclusion of a high percentage of the population belonging to minority groups in the United States.

6. Presence in the medical field: We see a low presence of professionals in healthcare who come from minority groups. There is no set proven route to recruit and guide new students from minority groups into healthcare because there are so many existing restrictions to access university education within career paths considered elite, such as medicine.

After looking at the six largest issues, it's easy to arrive to the conclusion that Latinos in the United States, especially those who are immigrants, are disproportionately challenged by these hurdles preventing them access to healthcare. We also know that minorities face similar problems. The year 2020 ushered the Covid-19 global pandemic and the nation was able to see firsthand how those inequalities brought more death and illness to the Latino and African American communities.

One of the things that bothered me the most while *Mami* was hospitalized before she passed away was her frustration at not being understood, a sentiment I shared. I stayed with *Mami* until the end and during that time I witnessed many other families who experienced the same plight. These are moments of end of life, of emergency, of horror in a hospital room, and not being able to say and understand precise words made everything much more difficult.

One of my mentors at the time, Texas Diversity Council Executive Board Chairman, Dr. Harry Gibbs, Director of Diversity and Inclusion at MD Anderson Cancer Center, was the one who helped me create the Healthcare Diversity Council. I did not have any type of credential in the healthcare and health services field, and I was afraid that for that reason I would not have the necessary profile to go talk to the right people. Dr. Gibbs said to me something that I remember to this day, "It takes all faces, all kinds of people, to make something like this happen."

It was then that Dr. Gibbs and I began to discuss the feasibility of this council. Not only did he give me all of his support but encouraged me in such an amazing way that I started to say to myself, *We will make it happen.*

And, yes, we did! Twelve months later we launched the Healthcare Diversity Council. Its strategy sought to incorporate all those hospitals and institutions dedicated to medicine and the health system as part of this council. During the earlier months, I also realized that it was not only medical professionals that we needed as allies, but also pharmaceutical companies with the inclusion of all ethnic groups in clinical trials, something that should be a standard in clinical trials but is not. The healthcare industry is a powerful and well-funded player whose services and products will always be needed. Therefore, it's of high relevance to address its diversity, equity and inclusion.

Dr. Gibbs gave me something wonderful at that time. I saw in him much more than a mentor, I found someone who believed in me, who supported me and lifted me up, always seeking to offer me his knowledge and ideas without even a tiny bit of self-interest. He was an African American educated at Harvard Medical School, so he understood perfectly what we needed to do. He told me, "Ángeles, if there was ever a moment when this had to be done, it is now; and if there is someone who has to do it, it is you. You already have a huge platform with the National Diversity Council, but now your focus must turn to this industry, the sleeping giant that was awakened by the Affordable Care Act, which all of a sudden managed to include millions of people in this country who had never had health insurance. But also, in the sociological aspect, demanded that the hospitals make a complete restructuring of their services to include the understanding and study of cultural, ethnic, religious and many other aspects of the diversity of their patients."

We did five conferences in different cities. Dr. Gibbs was the keynote speaker in each one of them. Participation was modest, but we had a large attendance of administrative and managerial staff.

One of the things that he and I agreed upon from the beginning was that to change the faces in healthcare we needed to create a program that would include students in the process of entering the health field. Not only to give them scholarships and support but to put them in contact with these administrators and executives who came to our conferences. We saw a lot of opportunity for information exchange. We wanted these two groups of people to get together for a variety of reasons. We wanted those already in the field to realize that a wave of color was coming and that these students were going to need support in order to graduate from STEM careers. Our message to them was that their companies benefited from being mentors.

Not too long after we launched our Council, Dr. Gibbs fell ill with cancer and passed away. However, I know he left this Earth feeling much joy because of everything he did to make this important program succeed.

The Council has grown and now has events and a presence in cities across the United States. We had our first national conference in 2019. To honor the memory of Dr. Gibbs we awarded the Dr. Harry Gibbs Jr. Legacy Award in Healthcare in recognition of individuals who in an extraordinary way have managed to stand out in their careers in healthcare, ensuring that their work will never be forgotten. It was very emotional for me because his entire family attended the conference. The most impressive thing about the conference was that we had so many students from all over Latin America. I told them, "I ask you to walk around this place and find your Dr. Gibbs." It was wonderful to see the students get up from their seats and come over to greet the doctors, nurses, administrators, and managers who were there. At that moment I not only saw *Mami's* dream come true but also

Dr. Gibbs's ideal, that to achieve something incredible you need all faces.

The conversation about the ravages of the 2020 pandemic in the Latino and immigrant communities is not new. We knew in advance that this was happening in the healthcare field. The objective now is to improve it so that innocent people stop suffering the consequences. The door to talk openly about the subject of discrimination, inequality, and access in healthcare was opened because of a global crisis. It's an opportunity we can't let go by. It's time to take down the virus of racism, xenophobia, and cultural incompetence.

Future doctors from minority communities at the first Healthcare Diversity Council Conference.

Winners of the Dr. Harry Gibbs Jr. Legacy Award in Healthcare.

First Healthcare Diversity Council Conference, in honor of Dr. Gibbs' memory.

"Quequis"

Ingredientes
- 2 tazas de harina
- 1 taza de azúcar
- 4 cucharaditas de royal
- 4 huevos
- ½ de leche
- 50 grs de mantequilla

Modo De Hacerse.

Se bate muy bien la mantequilla hasta que esponje enseguida se agrega el azúcar y los huevos, se sigue batiendo por separado debe cernirse el harina con el royal se agrega a lo que ya tenemos batido poniéndole suficiente leche para que quede una pasta de quequis, se engrasan muy bien los mol-

The Circle of Influence

"It's not so much about the people you know, but about the people who want to meet you and learn from you."

As a woman in Corporate America, and even more so as an immigrant, I realized it was important that I sought after and integrated into my life a select group of people I admired and that I could reach out to at any given moment, in particular when I needed career advice. I call them my "circle of influence" and they are my tribe, my executive decision board. Their knowledge, their presence and their advice are a real treasure, especially when hitting uncertain times. That's why I believe all of us should have a circle of influence.

On the other side of the coin, we should be aware of the fact that we are always role-modeling for others and influencing other people. People we know and people we don't know. That's why as a Latina and an immigrant in a position of power I'm always checking myself to motivate and encourage through my words and my actions.

It's important to point out that in my specific case I've always been extremely thankful to the United States for every single opportunity it has given me. I know that I've had to jump through hoops and hurdles, that I've dealt with rejection at every step, that I've had to stay silent in the face of insulting words, but even after all that the results are spectacular. This life and this career that I've earned through small victories and big accomplishments came at a great cost, but it would've never been possible in México. It's sad, but it's true. I worked hard to reach for the stars in the United States, because I knew that goal was possible with great perseverance, enthusiasm, and determination. This is the flag of hope all immigrants drape themselves in, we know we can, *sí se puede*, that when we give it our all everything is possible.

When I travel, I spend time with many immigrants who are women. I got to say that I'm always joyfully impressed by the tenacity and the resilient spirit I find in each one of them. We, Latina women, are natural entrepreneurs, we will always find an opportunity to rise; and if we don't, we will come up with something. We are ambitious, strong, and stubborn. Sometimes the big break is in front of us, and other times we'll go into the dark searching for it. There's nothing that will stop us. We are not afraid of starting at the bottom because from there the only way is up. We have already surpassed so many obstacles before coming to the United States, and hundreds more after arriving, we know how to take a few ingredients and make it into something of value.

I also believe with all my heart that it is not so much about who I know but about those who want to get to know me. That's why for most of us our first circle of influence will be comprised by the people who will help us up the first steps in our journey. Afterwards, when we get to a higher level, we can become part of another circle of influence and help others climb up. We are all drops that fall and create circles, touching others and creating larger and larger circles within circles in such a harmonious way that, before we realize it, together we turn into an ocean, and united in our efforts we become that giant wave that creates change and hope.

I am committed to being accessible to other people. When someone connects with me, asks me a question, or requests my support, instead of feeling the annoyance of answering so many messages in any given day, I put myself in that person's shoes and understand that perhaps I can help in some way. I receive between one hundred and one hundred and fifty messages a day, only on LinkedIn, so it is not easy to read and answer all, but I have also learned that in my vocabulary there is the word "no" and I shouldn't be ashamed to use it when necessary.

I have been lucky to be surrounded by many influential women in my life. During my corporate career it was mostly men who helped me achieve my goals and encouraged me to keep climbing. However, when it comes to my personal and spiritual life, I can honestly say that the people who influence and inspire me have always been women. When I lost *Mami* I felt that not only had I just lost the most influential person in my life, which she was, but that I had in a way lost part of me. I was incomplete. And it was not until then that I realized that as women we have the ability to be our best allies. Although many times we do not support each other the way we should, when each of us manages to find their circle of friends, we feel a joy like nothing else on earth.

To me, influence means that these are the people who have helped me become who I am. Any of us may know and interact with dozens, maybe even hundreds of people daily. But we need to identify and differentiate between those who are true part of our life, the people whose advice we will take because it comes from a genuine place, and those who are close to us because of a specific goal.

With this in mind, I think of three fabulous Latinas that I admire and in whom I find a tremendous source of inspiration. And I think of them because, like me, they are immigrants who had to fight a hundred times more for each of their achievements. Every single one of them came into my life and became an important part of it.

Pilar Ortiz is a journalist who emigrated from Colombia. For two decades she was the anchor and news director of the most important newscast at *Univision*, Tampa. She's also been a producer for news outlets such as *CBS Telenoticias, Univision, Caracol, RCN* and *24 Horas*. Today, she trains clients to communicate at events, conferences, or in front of a camera more effectively.

I met Pilar when our organization hired her to be the mistress of ceremonies for the Latino Leadership Awards at the National Diversity Council in Miami. Since then, she's worked with me and my staff at several events that've taken place in Miami, San Antonio, Los Angeles and México City, some times as MC, others as moderator and even as panelist at a virtual event in 2020.

I remember one day we were talking, and Pilar was admiring a necklace I was wearing with a pearly white firefly on one side and green overtones on the other. She said she thought it was beautiful. So, without thinking about it, I took it off and gave it to her. I told her that I would explain later why I was doing that. Shortly after, I sent her an email telling her that my grandmother always told me that each of us can shine from the inside, like a firefly. And added that that was a teaching that I literally carry in my heart wherever I go. What's more, I collect accessories of all kinds that carry fireflies and when I see an opportunity to leave those words with some other woman, I do so. Among immigrant women we can support each other to the point of making the inner glow of each one shine brightly, especially in those moments of darkness where together we can light the way.

Pilar is a very generous woman. She utilizes her own time to share her experience with others. She has supported me tremendously over the years and the two of us have grown together, adding to our experience and our wisdom through our interactions, especially in those times when we were developing a new council, the Council for Latino Workplace Equity, which will lead us to continue pushing for equity for Latinos in their jobs and careers.

As a career journalist and an experienced entrepreneur in the communications field, Pilar participates in forums, boards of directors and conversations that generate useful and necessary discussions. She does this by facilitating conversations, moderating panels, and conducting interviews. She always says, "The important thing is to develop empathy, to listen actively and not to judge someone who is different. It is useless to spend time criticizing. We all have a long way to go. We can change the story we want to tell about ourselves without becoming victims but rather always defending those who are voiceless. Knowledge (internal and of the environment) and education are the two tools that will allow us to bridge the gap. I think that part of the solution is to speak assertively to generate change."

Pilar inspires me to be better. She sees the genius in each of us. Through her work and now most recently in her book, *"El genio de la botella,"* she helps each person recognize their greatness, see their worth, gain self-confidence and learn to shine.

I know that I can count on Pilar always and for everything. We support each other because that's what a good friend does; even more so when we understand that as immigrant women and leaders what we do together will have a multiplier effect that will impact many people, including those who will somehow benefit from our work beyond participating in an event. Just as *Mami* influenced me, now it's up to us to take that shared wisdom as far as possible.

Cecilia Orellana-Rojas is a sociologist and diversity expert from Chile. I met her during a presentation we made at AT&T to secure the corporate sponsorship of the telecommunications giant. Cecilia was one of the first people in the United States who told me that I must stop apologizing for who I am, for my English with a foreign accent, and hold my head high or else people would always "put me in my place." She was a leader on diversity at AT&T and one of the few Latina women who had already excelled on diversity and inclusion decades ago.

Her passion for diversity led her to play a significant role in our organization when we established the Texas Diversity Council. She helped organize, plan and execute Dennis' vision. She took on the role as our council president in San Antonio and was founding member of the Texas Hispanic/Latino Summit, establishing its mission as a space for Hispanic voices within the Texas Leadership and Diversity Conference.

Cecilia is a very smart and extremely astute woman when it comes to setting strategy, developing a plan and implementing everything flawlessly. There is mutual respect between us since, after leaving the corporate world, she chose to join me as vice president of strategy and research for the National Diversity Council.

To me, Cecilia is a pillar of stability in my life. She always has the right words to help me decide how to best move forward. But above all, she has become a friend so present, so intimate in my life, that I see her as the sister I lost. And that is priceless.

Of the three women I mention in this chapter, Cecilia is the one who lives in San Antonio and with whom I have spent the most time. Cecilia has been my right arm and a particularly valuable guide in my growth as a person, mother, executive and sister. The two of us complement each other. We laugh at the times when I am thinking of calling her, suddenly the phone rings and it's her on the line. We are so in sync that it's a little unreal the way things happen. As a good Chilean, she taught me the love for wine, since Chile is undoubtedly a country with wonderful vineyards and wines.

Cecilia is the sister I lost and the aunt that my children love dearly. On a professional level, we both know the topic of diversity, equity and inclusion so well that we could even recite it in our dreams. Over the years, our professional ties and personal friendship have become extraordinarily strong. Every time I remember how difficult it has been to navigate life by myself in a different country, I don't know what I would have done without the unconditional support of Cecilia, always loyal, always present in difficult moments and also in moments of immense joy. Having this level of support is, without a doubt, the best gift that life can give to anyone.

At the time I was writing this book, Cecilia was in Chile saying goodbye to her mother, a wonderful woman I called *tía*, auntie, for many years. Today, as we have both lost our mothers, we have even more history that bring us together. I've always said it and I'll repeat it: We are the continuation of our mothers, we are their voices today and tomorrow, we are everything we are because they loved us.

**Ani Palacios** came into my life during the first years of the Texas Diversity Council. She is a journalist and communicator who emigrated from Perú decades ago and was working at the time as a community outreach supervisor for Nationwide Insurance, Texas region. She'd always tell me that I made her feel peace, tranquility, and a lot of love. I'd reply to her that I loved her energy.

Shortly after arriving in San Antonio, she published her first novel and then won her first International Latino Book Award, with the distinction of obtaining the recognition for best novel and the worth noting fact that bestseller Paulo Coelho took second place, behind her, in that contest. It did not take long for her to leave the giant check of the corporation to completely dedicate herself to writing and publishing; her main goal to this day is to discover and promote new voices of Spanish literature in the United States and around the world, offering that talent access to the same editorial services as known authors.

Papi was one of her most enthusiastic fans. Ever since I brought him Ani's first novel, he never tired of asking me when the next one was coming out. It always inspired me to see her take difficult, sometimes controversial positions, standing firm until she'd reached her objectives. She can be pensive and creative, but when she sets goals, I've never seen Ani be deterred by obstacles or challenges.

We have known each other for more than fifteen years and even though she's now a highly recognized author, her essence has not changed. She is a brilliant writer. She has to her credit twelve International Latino Book Awards, three of them for best novel, she is a member of the Indiana / Purdue Delegation of the North American Academy of the Spanish Language, she's been chosen as part of the New Latino Boom movement of authors in the United States, has been recognized as a successful immigrant in the book "How They Made It in America" and has already published 150 books through her company, Pukiyari Editores/Publishers. Nevertheless, Ani continues to look for ways to express herself, to capture the essence of her characters, to convey emotions, often using immigrant and professional women as protagonists in her novels. And she continues to fight for the ideals that brought her to the United States, for diversity, fairness, and inclusion. It's because of how much I appreciate her —professionally, as an immigrant Latina, as a writer, and as a friend—, that when the time came to write and publish my book, I had no doubt I wanted Ani in my team as my editor and my publisher. We had a blast and learned so much!!!

Ani Palacios during her first media tour for her first novel, "Nos vemos en Purgatorio," in Lima, Perú.

Posing with Pilar Ortiz and her new book,
"El genio de la botella".

With Cecilia Orellana-Rojas, standing by my side,
and Mrs. Kennedy, seated in front of me, at the
Global Diversity Council, México City.

23. Rollito de Carne y Jamón

Ingredientes

1/4 de carne de preferencia de filete o aguayón
1 lata de jamón
1 cebolla - tomate
tantita sal y harina 5 pimientos
1 1/2 taza de vinagre
manteca

Modo de hacerse

Se muelen las especies y se agrega con el vinagre la carne se sala y se pone en lo que ya tenemos molido se deja se deja reposar media hora por separado se muelen 2 tomates asados después de ese tiempo se saca la carne y se unta manteca y en seguida el jamón se enrolla asegurándose con un hilo para que apriete y se re-

My Second Mom

"Don't punish yourself if you end up missing some of your kid's activities. But when you do attend, make sure you are truly present because they'll know.".

Dennis Kennedy's mother, who also lives in San Antonio, has been, since we met, a person who always treated me like a daughter. When I lost *Mami*, Mrs. Kennedy started to play a loving role of mother to me and of grandmother to my children.

Mrs. Kennedy is the woman through which my mom connects with me, with my soul, to this day. When she talks to me or offers me advice, even the way she speaks to me or the words she uses to guide me, remind me of my mother. I feel she represents my mother's voice.

Not only did she become my second mother, but also took on the role of the woman that I will seek when I have questions or concerns that only another mother would know and understand. Just like me, she's the mother of three boys. And she's been an extraordinary mother to them. Whenever I need advice on something regarding my boys, I'd find myself reaching out to her.

My kids were extremely active growing up. For instance, Tony was a star athlete at school and a classical music tenor that sang in multiple languages. I felt guilty whenever I had to travel for work and missed out on his recitals or his games. But Mrs. Kennedy would go to everything, she was part of their lives and a great influence in their daily routine. Her consistent presence helped me deal with my own insecurity as a single mother who traveled way too much. She became their loving grandmother, making time for anything they would need and to unconditionally offer me her emotional support when I felt like venting or discussing something.

One time I confessed to her that I was feeling extremely guilty for all the activities and events I constantly missed. I told her I wanted to be there for them since my sons were always making me so proud. She told me, "You know, Ángeles, it's not about being at every single occasion, it's about being one hundred percent present when you're able to make it. Don't blame yourself for what you can't attend, but make sure they know you are there when you are there." I'd love for every woman out there to understand the point she was trying to make. It's about being completely focused on our children and unplugged from everything else when we are with them. When any of us is able to reach this type of connection, it makes us feel at peace, and harmony will come into our lives.

Another thing that I observed with my mom but heard from Mrs. Kennedy is that it's important to always feel grateful, especially for the good things life brings. And when something bad occurs, to be able to recognize what's happening while trying to balance out the negative with the positive. Learning to have a heart filled with gratefulness help us see the positive but it's also a path to staying mainly in a state of happiness. Understanding this helped me answer, maybe in a different way, that question I always had about my mother, *How is it possible that Mami, having so little, is so happy? Does she not have any ambition in life?* It was not like that at all. I realized that gratitude brings happiness, and that's the way my mom saw everything.

Mrs. Kennedy also has a fantastic and contagious sense of humor. When my kids visited with her, they'd always came home happy. She spoiled them like a real loving grandma and took them out for meals and wonderful day trips. In her I saw the fabulous grandmother my mom could've continue being to my boys.

She gave me all the advice I needed and that only a mother can provide. There was this time when my child was performing poorly at a football game. He lost every play, he was not focused and he was making a lot of mistakes. In Texas this sport is like a religion and parents take it very seriously. I was incredibly nervous because I saw that my son was failing his team, and everything was going very wrong. Mrs. Kennedy, with the extreme patience that characterizes her, took me by the hand and told me that everything was going to be fine. But nothing changed, and as the game entered the second half, my son was making even more mistakes. Sitting in the stands I noticed that the parents of the other players were looking at me with annoyance and I felt a lot of pressure. So, without thinking about it, I got up and yelled at my son, told him to wake up or I would take him out of the game and out of that sport if he didn't play as he should. At that moment Mrs. Kennedy grabbed me by the arm, made me sit down, looked at me very seriously and said something I will never forget, "Because of being Latino, your son has already been labeled as someone who cannot be trusted. His teammates and his coach are biased against him because this is "not his sport." Never, listen to me please, never show him that you doubt him or that you don't believe in him. He will hear that from everyone, but his mother should be the exception to that rule." Uffff... what a great and important lesson she taught me! My children have always heard from her nothing but words of encouragement and have felt her unconditional love as a grandmother.

If I close my eyes and go through my past trying to see the people who were consistently part of my life, both in the greatest joys and the deepest sorrows, Mrs. Kennedy is there, holding my hand in all those moments. She has been to all my meetings, all my conferences, every graduation, first communion and birthday celebration... everything. Her love as mother and grandmother to me and my children appeared suddenly, without me ever asking. I am so grateful to her because being an immigrant, like so many women, I left everything: my family, the people I loved, my country, my culture... I don't have anyone else in San Antonio. That's why for me it is a joy that I found in this country the opportunity to have a second mother, to have her for so many years, to love her deeply. My children and I feel unconditional love with her. When Tony got his driver's license, the first thing he said to me was, "Mommy, I'm going to see Mrs. Kennedy and take her for a ride in my car." There are tons of stories like this one! She has shared all those special family moments.

We never know how those people who will influence our lives so much are going to come to us. I never thought that I would have a Mexican mom and a second mom that is African American. I never thought I would learn so much about the struggle of African Americans in this country. She has told me many stories of what it was like for her to grow up in a place where there was so much rejection of her race, where there was slavery, where they had to fight so much to be "almost normal" and to be treated as human beings.

We are also bonded over the fact that we both are Catholic. It is not common in the United States for an African American to be Catholic, but she is. One of the things she has shared with me spiritually and religiously is her love for her church, the only African American Catholic church in San Antonio. I love going a couple of times a month with the boys to their mass. Even the father in that parish has become an important spiritual guide for me. The Very Rev. Kevin Fausz does not mince words ever and speaks with fierce resolution and conviction about the subjects he brings up.

There are no words to describe the gift that having Mrs. Kennedy in my life is to me. The respect, the love, the affection I have for her, the regard for the support she gave Dennis and me when we started the council. She has been a part of my life for almost twenty years now. I am grateful that in the times we live, in a country where minorities are pitted against each other, I've learned so much from her and her achievements in this matter. My wish is that every person out there finds their Mrs. Kennedy.

In her seventies now, Mrs. Kennedy is still incredibly active, she goes out, she drives herself everywhere, she dresses like a queen, always perfect and beautiful, she is involved in many charitable causes. Seeing her every Christmas serving food to those who are not as fortunate is incredible. For many years she has invited soldiers from the San Antonio military base to her Thanksgiving dinner. She brings six soldiers who are far from

home and otherwise would be alone during the holiday to share her table.

I'm so used to talking with her all the time. It's such a joy! She was an elementary school teacher for many years and, just like me, has a love for reading and staying informed about current events. I've learned so much from her, from her great heart of service, from her unwavering Catholic faith. I have learned so much about the true African American community, its suffering, its longing for justice, and its struggles.

There's a yearning in her voice when she talks about the past, but she's never bitter or negative. She knows that everything she has had in her life has been because of her effort and love for her children. Like me, her dedication to them is unshakable. And whenever she has the opportunity, she tells me stories about her boys when they were kids, their antics and how much she loves having them as her children.

When we open our hearts and focus on seeking the best of every person, we attract some of that great energy. I think that's what happened when Mrs. Kennedy and I started this long-lasting relationship. I love it when we are somewhere and someone asks how we know each other, and she says she's my mother and I say I'm her daughter.

24 Rollitos de Carne en frío
150 grs. Carne de res
150 grs. Carne puerco
50 grs. Tosino
10 grs. Chorizo
1 Clara de huevo
ejotes y zanahoria en tiritas
2 ajos
1 pedazo de ceballa
yerbas de olor (mejorana laurel tomillo)
3 grs. Jamón
1 latita de Chile

Manera de hacerse.

Se fríe el tosino enseguida el chorizo picado agregando la carne, revuelta con la clara de huevo y sal (se le revuelve a la carne) se retira del fuego y se extiende en un lienzo húmedo poniéndole tiritas de jamón zanahoria ejote y chile se en

Diversity-Equity-Inclusion

*"Treat others as they would
like to be treated."*

When I look at my whole life, my path, my obstacles, my challenges, my achievements, my moments of defeat and those of joy, the tears shed and the smiles of pride, I realize that everything, down to the smallest detail, has served to offer me a unique perspective on the issues of diversity, equity and inclusion to which I have dedicated not only my career but also every beat of my heart.

As an immigrant, it has meant a great deal to me to have been given a voice of authority as a subject matter expert on DEI. I find myself humbled when I take stock at the impact of my contributions to this important cause.

The historical events of the year 2020 presented us with an extraordinary opportunity to bring to the forefront issues that until then were taboo in many circles. Health inequalities during the pandemic, national and global protests sparked by George Floyd's murder during his arrest, led to an explosion of testimonies and conversations about police violence in dealing with minorities, and especially with African American men, as well as unequal treatment in front of the law... all this forced us to examine once again who we are as a country in the United States, what are our values, what is our legacy, what is expected of a developed nation, how young people are using their voices to influence our way of seeing things.

What happened in 2020 put the country in front of the mirror. It forced us to stare at each other naked for a long and uncomfortable period. It reflected to us the realities of inequalities, which tend to become more visible and horrifying in times of crisis.

Before, in the field of diversity and inclusion, there was little discussion about social or racial justice. These issues are centerstage today because of what we went through as a nation in 2020. It horrified us and stirred a collective sense of shame and rage. Many CEOs now want to have that conversation, they choose to dive deeper than ever to understand the context and history of injustices experienced by their employees, their customers, their neighbors. By doing that, they are empowering themselves to become allies who seek solutions.

Everything that happened in 2020 changed the focus to one that demands greater depth in conversations and an urgency for societal evolution as we have not seen for a long time.

From my point of view, the fundamental concepts of diversity, equity and inclusion are interrelated, and I can understand them in depth because they point to key moments in my own history as an immigrant, a Latina and a professional. I faced firsthand what it means to be an immigrant in this country, what it means to be a woman of color (the term used in the United States, although Latinos are of all races and colors), what it means to be labeled with stereotypes created to define a group of people in a generalized, derogatory and oppressive way.

For me, living those experiences as a woman, as an immigrant who arrived in this country, was both shocking and remarkable. There came a time when I realized that I was a poster child for diversity and inclusion. I represented all that I was witnessing and living.

When I reached this conclusion in an observational and introspective way, the desire to promote in myself and in others the self-awareness of who we are, how we see the world, and what we want from life, grew exponentially. At the same time, it was then that I was curious to understand how this process of self-awareness manifests itself in an organization. Knowing that I was different in so many dimensions helped me realize I was unique in this country, exploring those features in myself taught me how to take advantage of all that I had and others didn't. Once I was able to clearly see everything that made me one of a kind, I never again saw my disadvantages because every tool at my disposal was an original with no other exact copies available in the market.

One of the most important features I brought with me when I arrived in the United States was cultural competence. I don't need anyone to tell me about Mexicans or Latinos. I grew up in that culture. I know it in depth, I respect it, I honor it, I feel proud of it. This is not something anyone can learn from a book or a course. These are the cultural elements Latino immigrants bring from their countries, and we know that we represent much more than the way we are depicted. Latin Americans come from one culture made from hundreds of cultures, with immense richness of history, cuisine, traditions, languages, folklore, and literature, among others. We recognize this from the time we are toddlers.

Upon arriving in the United States, and then starting my professional career, I quickly grasped that there were many aspects about myself that gave me certain advantage. Those singularities became my tools of success, as I was able to use them to recognize in a special way many things that others could not see. Even my perspective was different, especially when it came to dealing with clients from different minority groups, immigrants from other countries and, very especially, Latino immigrants. I understood the added value that my personal experience brought into my interaction with clients. For example, in my first job, I had colleagues and supervisors who complained that I was taking "too long" on calls with clients who spoke in Spanish, but what I saw was the opportunity to treat them the way they wanted to be treated, make a true connection, and set the relationship in a way that ensured they would be customers for life. However, since in Latino culture it is considered rude to go straight to the business in hand, the set-up required an extensive preamble during the call where we would talk about the client's personal life. A few minutes for a lifetime client. Not bad at all.

Let me brag a tiny bit. At my very first job in the United States, with a company that sold IBM products, not only was I the one who generated the most sales within my team, but also left my mark in their process. Of course, they complained at first about my lengthy sales calls, but as soon as they realized that my clients were loyal because of the way I treated them, with respect and regard, they incorporated my method to their system.

I was able to show them that embracing the unique aspects of each person we deal with helps to expand the business and become known to more clients in that industry. They saw that honoring the diversity of a person in an effective way achieves results, especially when we integrate those ideas into our other teams, when we create more efficient communication with our target groups, when we expand our message to reach new clients, when we hire people of the communities we want to approach, market and sell. It was important to me that they could discover for themselves that I did all this work, that they saw at the beginning as an extra, not because I had a good heart but because that's the way we Latinos are programmed, especially those of us who are immigrants.

Looking in from the outside, I was able to immediately see what the company was lacking and how that deficiency would unknowingly place them on a path of failure. One simple step: understanding their clients' actual diversity, their humanity, would surely open the door to inclusion, to acceptance and to a comfortable space where their clients and providers felt they belonged.

I've mentally gone back many times to the lessons I learned in school and college in México, the country where I was taught about values, principles, empathy, and cultural differences. I remember being in elementary school and having guests from a foreign country. We were taught that someone who didn't grew up in our country didn't necessarily know everything about our traditions and our Mexican culture and national identity; and that it was our civic duty to honor them as they were and to teach them and guide them, without ever making fun of them, so they'd felt included.

I'm not denying there's racism in our Latin American countries. However, I feel that discrimination and ethnic rejection is more aggressive and profoundly embedded in the United States.

It wasn't until I got here that I understood for the first time in my life how harmful it is to be a victim of racism: how it hurt me, how it made me feel inferior… And I also realized how easy it would've been to be marked forever, even damaged at my core level and self-esteem, if I hadn't had a deep knowledge of who I am, of my cultural heritage, of the contributions of people like me to this country. Therefore, as a professional, it was always imperative to me that when someone said something racist, I made them understand, in a simple but firm way, the context and the history of the words they were using or why when they say something like that it is hurtful and harmful. I'd find a way to use the situations to help others understand those who are not like them. In my mind I'd say, *They have no idea of what they are doing,* and I'd focus on the goal, which is the change of perspective and, therefore, of attitude. We start from the idea that people are not bad, that they simply have no idea how awful they look and how much damage they do when they behave in a derogatory way towards other human beings whom they do not even know.

When I arrived in the United States, it was a culture shock for me to feel how distant the conversations were, how cold the way of doing business was. It was like everything was a transaction rather than a win-win relationship that could continue to develop in the long run. Years after I left the first company where I worked, the supervisor would call me and tell me that the clients with whom I had a relationship were still with them and were asking about me. That's making a positive impact wherever you go!

I am deeply passionate about diversity, especially the cultural diversity that all immigrants bring. In some way we contribute a lot to relationships, dynamics, teams, the communities where we live and the country that welcomes us. For example, we must remember that we also had slavery in Latin American countries and, therefore, an immense cultural legacy that is part of our national formative experience. I grew up surrounded by Afro descendants in my community. I love the story of Gaspar Yanga, considered one of the first liberators of slaves in the Americas (the continent, not the US). That is why I see them as a part of me and such an important part of our cultural identity. However, Latinos should not be defined by color, as I have mentioned before, we are every race and every color. When we use the label or term "brown" we are excluding many of our own —in my opinion, we should not allow this to continue.

It was interesting for me to understand that certain words that are used in our countries in a loving way, can ring offensive in the US. For example: It's common in Latin American countries to nickname people based on physical qualities. My mother affectionately called me *Negrita* (which would translate to dark-skinned), and I did not understand how something that I appreciated so much, because it came from *Mami's* heart, was suddenly a bad word in the United States, a shameful and offensive word. This example teaches us how words can be the same and mean opposite things in different places.

On their own, differences are not bad nor good. They are simply that: differences. It's when we learn to take them to the next level that differences can make us tougher and capable of adapting to diverse environments while helping us develop a healthier disposition to establish stronger, deeper and lasting relationships.

If we start from the idea that diversity exists and that we are all different in many aspects (physical, intellectual, emotional, cultural, educational and many more dimensions); and if instead of seeing this as a negative, we accept it as a natural part of the fabric of a society and we decide to respect the perspective of those around us by listening to them with an open mind, we will see that these differences are what make us strong as a community, as an organization, as a country.

But diversity in itself is not enough. The successful recipe has three ingredients: diversity, equity, inclusion.

Equity means that there is a willingness to treat all people the same, without discrimination, but considering their personal situations. The types of equity can be numerous: gender equity, social equity and more. Basically, it is the Platinum Rule: *"Treat others as they would like to be treated."*

Inclusion is the last of these three ingredients; it's the one that provides the space for diversity and equity, which organizations now manage in an increasingly natural and organic way, to allow the inclusion of everyone in the organization by making a mix that leads to good results.

In a workplace context diversity is, "I invite you to come to work here"; equity is, "I give you the same opportunities as everyone else to develop yourself and I pay you the same salary for the same job"; and inclusion is, "I invite you to the table, I listen to you, and I consider your opinions. Here, you belong as you are."

Many organizations do not even reach diversity voluntarily. In many cases, a crisis is what prompts transformation. Lately we've started to see an interesting change. Due to population shifts with respect to available workers, and the fact that Baby Boomers are retiring and there are not enough white workers to replace them, we have begun to see that a greater number of workers from minority groups are organically entering organizations.

The new generations are also bringing much more diversity into the workforce. We saw some of this with Gen X. Later, Millennials revolutionized and increased those changes, adding to the mix groups that were marginalized and unrecognized in the past. Now, with Gen Z, there are five vastly different generational populations working together, going through some clashes and, most importantly, evolving the workplace landscape.

The organizations that did not prepare to receive such a diverse workforce, are now in crisis and do not know what to do. The rigid cultures of these organizations create internal conflicts because they are neither designed, nor prepared, nor willing to understand the socio-cultural changes that are occurring around them. The changes will continue, and organizations need to catch up and keep catching up. If an organization is not ready, it will be left behind, or, in the best of cases, it will become a revolving door where diverse people enter and quickly leave because they see that in that workplace they will have neither equity nor inclusion; and if someone stays, the most likely scenario is that they will be unhappy and in a short time apathy will overtake them.

In some cases, the organization may have great diversity in the lower echelons, but as we go up, fewer and fewer diverse people are found, and it is predominantly Anglo individuals who hold senior management positions. We find minimal diversity at the top, certainly not enough to create change within corporate culture.

The truth is that currently there is no organization that has established the three ingredients in a solid and stable way.

Studies of equity and diversity at the managerial level in the United States reveal how much diversity exists in the C Suite, or management, and what kind of diversity it is. Many organizations consider that they have reached the highest goal if they have an Anglo-American woman in an executive position. The reality is that they are on the lowest rung and still have a long way to go if there's no representation of women from other groups or individuals from different minorities.

Something that I have observed that happens frequently is that an organization will take action on diversity, equity and inclusion when it has external pressure to do so. It's almost unheard of that an organization will seek to change on their own because they had a moment of enlightenment and suddenly realized that diversity means business. The most likely situation involves a huge public relations crisis, public pressure, and a rush to "patch" the problem and make it disappear, in that order. We saw the perfect example in 2020 with the murder of George Floyd, an African American man, at the hands of abusive police officers. Afterwards, many cities named streets and plazas Black Lives Matter. It's a wonderful gesture but doesn't fix the underlying problem.

Normally, the depth to which organizations are willing to go in terms of getting educated about different minority groups does not go beyond the basics. For example, it does not dare going deeper and study the historical and prevalent problems between different minorities. During my career I have always sought to have all the resources available so that we can swim as far from the shore in the conversation as the executives of the organizations are ready to go.

Even with all the diverse workers available and generational attitude shifts, I still come across so many executives who tell me that "they can't find diverse candidates." The willingness to do so is what's lacking here, because, although it is overwhelming to always be looking for excuses, I see that it is easier for them to say why they have not done it than to look for ways to solve their deficiencies. They say it is a matter of additional expenses, or that they do not see hiring diverse candidates as good ROI. I think it's also a matter of feeling embarrassed when looking in the mirror and acknowledging that they are doing something wrong. Unfortunately, most of the time, something serious and publicly embarrassing must happen to twist their arm into saying they will. Perhaps in the moment they manage to realize that if they do not do it, something even more horrendous, more visible, more expensive to fix could happen. We may get them to let us guide them during the crisis, but once the event has passed and they are no longer holding a hot potato in their hands, especially when the media turns the page and turn their attention to another story, the problem may return if the changes are only cosmetic. Organizations that willfully ignore foundational problems end up with problems everywhere. When looking for a solution we will find resistance coming from the executives and sometimes even from the employees. Many feel that there is no reason to change, they think that it's a waste of energy and resources. Honestly, they cannot find a reason for change because they are too deep in the thick of it to see anything. Also, their reluctance to act may be caused by an irrational fear of being told that they are guilty of everything that has happened.

One thing is for sure: unless we can count on all the white executives as part of those conversations as true allies, not much will change. They must be part of the conversation, the development of the strategy and the execution of it. They must be convinced of the need for change. It is not easy to get to this point. Often, they feel attacked. They think that the conversation about "white privilege" makes them look bad. Once all the cards are put on the table, they can no longer just say that they promote diversity, equity and inclusion in their organization without someone holding them accountable for their words. These are often loud and explosive conversations; it pushes them out of their comfort zone and influence; it exposes them, faults and all, in front of other leaders; it forces them to say out loud, "All these things were happening under my authority and my command. Not only do they reflect badly on the organization, but they also reflect poorly on me as a person." Nobody likes to do that kind of exercise. These are delicate steps. But with a lot of work, it is possible to explore the "truth" of that organization on these issues and develop a way to fix those mistakes for the benefit of all.

During 2020, and in large part due to the massive protests against racism, we have seen that many CEOs have risen up and have publicly stated that what is happening is not only unacceptable but have also acknowledged to being part of the problem. They state that institutional racism has been around for too long, but now that they understand it, they must change. What usually happens behind the scenes is that their own employees take a fateful event, and the ensuing social movement, as the catalyst to open up the channels of communication and call for that long-needed change. In addition, executives may take interest at these forward-looking renovations since there may be at stake millions of dollars coming from diverse customers and communities, and because they see that they need those diverse employees to keep moving in the right direction.

There are moments in history that become an awakening event for large segments of the population. Special times when all of us stop and say, "This is not right. Racism should not exist in our society." In the same way, organizations also come to the conclusion that if they remain as they are it is quite possible that their competition, which is perhaps doing a much better job in those fields, will also end up surpassing them in the areas of innovation and longevity. Diversity, equity and inclusion create workspaces where the future is seen, everyone's ideas are valued and those who stand out are rewarded.

Finally, it is also important to dedicate a few lines to the issue of racism and discrimination among minorities. I see it this way: we are all programmed from a young age to feel that we have to compete for the things we want. Now, when this competition occurs between minority groups, the general thought we've come to believe is that only one group can win, since there's too little to share. We have become used to competing against each other, instead of demanding more opportunities. For example, they tell us that there is only one high-level position for a minority. Well, instead of destroying each other to take that position, we must ask why only one. We must unite and ask that they give us ten positions. We've been for years conditioned to believe a lie. Now we need to stand up together for what's right. We should never fight for the one chair we've been told is generously there for "someone like us." We must instead build a bigger table and place several chairs there for all of us. We must change the story to one that fits our goals and aspirations. We must learn to demand equality everywhere. And instead of remaining divided, we must unite and speak up, demanding opportunities for every one that deserves them.

We also must fight against the appearance of "something being done" when it's not done in an equitable fashion. I have started to see a pattern on the appointment of Black Chief Diversity Officers across the nation. If we take inventory in organizations, in most cases almost all the higher-ranking positions in DEI are entrusted to an African American executive. Yet, by doing this it leaves out all "others" to feel invisible, passed over and frustrated. When we look closely at the positions of DEI, we realize that those given the position are in turn hiring people that look just like them. The question becomes, *Isn't that what we are fighting against? Isn't this following the same pattern?* A diversity team cannot only be representative of one ethnic minority, it must be comprised of all of them. I take great pride in the fact that my team is representative of the communities that we champion and advocate: Native and Indigenous, LGBTQ-A, Black, Latino, Asian, Muslim, veteran, women, different abilities, etc.

As minorities we have become more aware of our own reality, and we have realized that they have been playing us against each other all this time. The opportunities have always been there, what happens is that we have never joined forces, we have not given that strong push together, we have not yelled, "Either all or nothing." Let's be mindful, though, that the concepts of diversity, equity and inclusion are fluid, and the dynamics will gradually transform according to the future groups and their needs. What may seem unattainable today will be normal tomorrow; then we will have other goals, other revolutions, other evolutions shaped by the new generations.

Women's Leadership Program, México.
Bringing this program to México City was very emotional to me. After a long time away, I was coming back to the country I love with an unbelievably valuable gift.

Women's Leadership Program, Dubai. Ever since I was a little girl, I was taught to recognize, honor and respect the culture and values of each community. That's why when traveling abroad, I'll purposely adhere to their customs and dress accordingly. It's my way of honoring their traditions. After this event, three high-ranking Latinas approached me and with tears in their eyes they hugged me and told me they never thought they would hear Spanish at a conference so far away from home.

Year 2015, United Kingdom. My welcome speech during the launching of our very first global program in London, sponsored by Kings College. A wonderful moment of pride for me, since this marks the day that our organization became international. It's my custom to always speak in the language of the country that is hosting me and also in Spanish, to honor my country of origin and my Hispanic heritage.

Rosas Carmela 2

Ingredientes

- 1 huevo
- ½ taza de azúcar
- ⅓ " " leche
- 375 gr de harina
- 4 cucharaditas royal
- 150 gr de manteca
- 2 cucharas de azúcar y canela

Modo de hacer

Se bate el huevo se le incorpora el azúcar la manteca después la harina y el royal y la leche se hecha en un molde y se le pone el azúcar encima

Fin

The Unsung Heroes

"The legacy of a true leader is to create more leaders and more opportunities."

Obstacles or not. Barriers or not. Walls or not. Latino immigrants, as well as the new generations and those who preceded us in the struggle, have always found the way to move forward, to triumph, to conquer new summits and to emerge victorious from the battle against multiple challenges. This can-do attitude comes from the environment of hope in which we grew up and the optimism with which we've learned to face adversity. It is in our DNA. We know how to get to our goals using fewer resources and looking for original avenues. The harsh realities of our countries of origin have taught us to create new paths where there are none. That is why it is so important to share with others our formulas for success and to proactively help those who are putting an effort in climbing the corporate ladder, become leaders in their organizations, or establish their businesses. It is not only about material progress but about pride in moving forward as a community.

"Creating a legacy requires building a path that can be taken by those who come after you in order to reach their own goals." That's an idea that I share frequently. As I've grown older, I've also developed a keen recognition of those who lighted my way. Every day now an urgency brews within me; it's the knowledge of the fact that the baton must pass to others, that the fight does not subside when any of us leaves.

Let's think of those women we admire so much as a giant wave that lifts everyone up when it stands up brave, its beautiful mantle decorated by the white foam encrusted with stories of so many daring fighters who were immortalized when they reached the shore.

To have this concept present in our daily lives is to connect the past with the future, making sure that the threads intersect, but never break.

We recognize so many universal heroes, but... who are the heroes and heroines of the Latino community in the US? They do exist, but we ought to learn to see them and thank them publicly.

From the beginning of our association, Dennis Kennedy was amazed at how little he saw the Latino community highlighting their own leaders with the enthusiasm they deserved. He'd always point to the fact that our many voices were missing from crucial conversations on the topics of diversity, equity and inclusion.

His comments made me wonder how little is known about our heroes and heroines. Many might assume that the only ones who have moved barriers are Mexicans and Cubans. We know that's not true, that we have always had representation and leaders that came from all Latino countries.

That was one of the main reasons why we formed a new council within the National Diversity Council, the Council for Latino Workplace Equity.

Latinos have had and continue to have a profound and positive influence in this country through our strong commitment to family, faith, hard work, and service to others. We have enhanced and shaped America's national character by adding these ingredients to it, and by also adding centuries-old traditions that reflect the multi-ethnic and multi-cultural dimensions of our community.

According to the updated 2018 US Census estimates, 62 million people or 18.7 percent of the population are of Hispanic or Latino origin. This represents a significant increase from the year 2000, which recorded the Hispanic population at 35.3 million or 13 percent. The number of Hispanic-owned businesses totaled 2.3 million in 2007 and the projected purchasing power of Latinos was $1.7 trillion for 2017. However, our representation in leadership roles and boardrooms in US businesses is still extremely low.

The purpose of the Council for Latino Workplace Equity is to seek inclusion for workers as well as the opportunity for Latino leaders to claim their place at the table with certainty and conviction. Within the framework of the National Diversity Council, we will leverage the incredible resources we have as a community to serve as a compass for our nation as we move forward with the next generation of Latino leaders in the United States.

Throughout my tenure with the National Diversity Council I've had wonderful opportunities to travel and get to know our people and our beautiful country while taking our programs and conferences to so many cities. Well, I'm an early riser and just love to go to the location where our conference will take place around five in the morning. I love to take a good look at the setup and make sure everything is in place. It's my preparation ritual. It helps me focus on the day. Typically, the conference starts at eight in the morning, but participants start arriving at seven. To me, one of the most joyful experiences as I walk through every room thinking of all the attendees who will be there soon, is the fact that the teams of workers I'll see at dawn are mostly comprised of Latinos, many of whom are immigrants employed in the hospitality field. They are the ones who are getting the tables ready, bringing out breakfast items, carrying coffee jugs and everything else needed to perfectly serve a large crowd. I always take time to welcome them and sit for a minute to savor a coffee. Most of the time one of the servers will also bring me an egg taco. That fills me with warmth and gives me so much and pride! Those brief exchanges remind me that when we connect with a person on a human level, at their level, where they know that we are part of them and they accept us because they see us as their equal, everything in that exchange is positively enhanced. I know this because when the conference starts and they realize that the person they served before is the person who is speaking on stage, the "boss," they smile. Immediately after, the look of joy, because I spoke to them in Spanish in the morning, turns into a look of appreciation and admiration. When I see that, I feel fulfilled. I know that that day I will speak with many "important" people, but it was my people who before the event nurtured me with a meal and helped me prepare emotionally to say what I have to say. It is also a practice of mine that when I am up and in front of the microphone and they are down and serving everyone who has come to the conference, I'll say in Spanish, "I want to thank those who are serving us today because, like me, they are immigrants, and they are doing a job that many do not know how to properly do or do not want to do at all."

Somehow in this country the word immigrant has a negative connotation. That is why it is so important that when one of us reaches a position where we have a platform, an audience, that we use it to provide context and educate those who do not understand the struggle of immigrants in the United States.

When I speak with the person who makes my bed at the hotel, or with someone who comes to remodel my house, or with the gardener... with immigrants who somehow are always ignored and unseen... and I ask, "What moves you to get up and do this every day?" Most of them answer, "Because I want my children to have a better life than mine." That right there is the immigrant's prayer. And it's mine. We all want our children to have a better life than the one we had, and we know that in this country we can find those opportunities for work, education, progress and so much more that we did not have in our countries of origin. Immigrants contribute a lot, but despite their immense presence they are invisible to most, they are the working ants that move everything, but few stop to recognize. I always say, "One good leader leaves many more leaders trained and ready for battle." I say this because the standard should be that after each one of us exits from leadership positions many more should be ready to step in, take the reins, and continue to improve the world.

I had the opportunity to give a speech at a conference to honor the legacy of Dr. Martin Luther King Jr. in 2015. When I came down from the stage an *imam* approached me, and after giving me his prayer of blessing, as is the custom, he said to me, "Why are you talking about MLK, who is gone, when there are so many Latino leaders that you should be talking about?" His words really touched me. They kept echoing in my mind weeks later. They were like the words of Dennis Kennedy, who always said to me, "Ángeles, why doesn't your community speak up, express itself out loud and to the public, saying what they want, just as we African Americans do? Why is it that they don't join forces? Why is it that they do not support each other?"

As I was meditating about it, I didn't try to ask *Why?* for that is just thinking about problems, but *Why not...?* which to me it is about looking for a solution.

The Council for Latino Workplace Equity was a project that we started in 2015 as an answer to those questions.

We have many individuals to look up to in our community, heroes and heroines who shaped our past. And at the same time, we have a large group of prepared Latinos, educated professionals, ready to undergo the necessary evolution to forge themselves into becoming our future leaders. The question is not only, *How do I move forward?* But, *How do I become a good leader and how many new leaders will I help rise with me?* And, once I'm at the top, *How can I help make the legacy of all those leaders recognized and become a permanent part of our history?*

Through the Council for Latino Workplace Equity, we try to move forward on all flanks. We advocate for the representation of Latino employees in different industries, so that people in our community are not thought of as those who go to the bottom of the pyramid, but rather as those who go in all positions, including the highest. It is important to be able to go to an organization, observe its composition, and ask, "Where are my people? Why are they not in the high-ranking levels? How do we get them to the higher positions?"

It is not until we raise our voices that we begin to move the needle of progress in favor of our own community. If others do not notice what we can see clearly, we must open their eyes so that they can appreciate the situation in its entirety, but also help them find a solution and be persistent in implementing it.

We look for Latino representation at all levels, as well as recognition of all the contributions of members of our community to all types of industries and sectors in this country.

For example, in Major League Baseball, a large number of players are Latino, but the organization that runs MLB has a very small number of Latinos on its management or executive board. This makes no sense! Through the council's work, we seek ways to ensure that Latinos are included at all levels in the workplace and that they benefit from their work and accomplishments. We also establish programs where we develop our Latino talent at all levels and promote it through the organizations associated with the council.

The Council for Latino Workplace Equity creates awareness. We know that our community is the largest minority with the greatest buying power in the United States, yet it is not taken into account when creating expansion plans and searching for management-level candidates.

Even when Latinos are recruited for high-level positions, the preference is to hire white Latinos who speak English and were raised in the United States. There's too much reluctance to give the opportunity to those Latinos of various races who speak both Spanish and English, albeit with a foreign accent, since they are mostly considered "not ready" or not "at the same level" as the other candidates.

The only way to convince a higher-up who thinks that way is by enlisting an ally in their circle of influence before showing up with a proposal. It should be someone who understands that an immigrant can be equal to or better than any of the other candidates considered for the position. Tech organizations, for example, were created by foreign professionals who studied their masters and doctorates in the United States and then stayed in the country to work. Those are organizations that are decades ahead of other sectors and industries. These are not easy conversations, but they are much more impacting when the benefit of making changes in terms of return on investment can be demonstrated.

I remember this one instance when I had to speak to the president of a university about this issue. We were in his office. He got up and going to the window pointed out a group of gardeners, all Latino, who were working on the lawn in front of the building. He said, "Ángeles, you see those wetbacks? I love those guys, they are good people, they work hard." I stared at him. I couldn't believe the words that came out of the mouth of a man in such an important position in an educational institution! I can justify the ignorance of a person who is not educated, who has not read, who has not exposed himself, who has not traveled... but how dare the president of a university use that word with me, a Latina of Mexican origin? I wanted to cry. My father was a *bracero*, someone who worked in the fields. When I looked at the workers down there being judged by this man from his ivory tower, I saw my dad, I saw my uncle, I saw people that I love. I was just starting my career with the Council but decided that I would much rather lose that account if it gave me the opportunity to educate that idiot who expressed himself in such an offensive way. I said, "Do you know how racist and how deeply painful those statements you just made are to me? You are not an ignorant person ... you are choosing to behave like an ignorant person." With his comments he wanted to tell me that he accepted diversity and that he liked Latinos. But what he really expressed to me was that he liked Latinos as long as they were subservient and worked as gardeners or in "low-level" positions, but not as university professors.

Understanding the mindset of the people we are trying to convince is very important in order to create a wise, coherent, productive strategy that will lead us to victory. That is why I am spending a lot of time today on developing groups of leaders to take command when people like me leave.

The Council for Latino Workplace Equity is dedicated not only to addressing the issue of equity for Latino workers in businesses and organizations, but it also seeks to recognize our communities' heroes and heroines. It is important that the mainstream public get to know our stories of struggle, perseverance and dedication. I want the stories of those who have contributed so much to this country to be known. Dr. Héctor P. García, for example, is a hero of our community, as a doctor, as a veteran, as a voice of influence in the White House who helped elect President Kennedy and who worked before MLK on issues pertaining civil rights ... but who is not widely known. Our children have no idea about the many Latino leaders who have done so much for this country, but their story has been almost forgotten. It's up to us to do that important job of knowing who our heroes are, both in the past and today. For example, through the Council we instituted the Dr. Héctor P. García Legacy Award in Leadership. We delivered it at our first conference where we managed to find and put under the same roof many leaders of our community in various sectors and representing the numerous countries throughout Latin America. This is a big difference from other events that generally only recognize members of the larger communities, mostly Mexican or Cuban. For us it was important that there was space and recognition for everyone since those stories are of the utmost importance for those who come later and need to find encouragement in someone like them. Truth is we are alike and when we see each other and are together we find and understand the strength that exists in the union of all our voices. That's why our event celebrates all Latin American countries, all equally, with everything we do, from putting flags on tables to entertainment and food.

    I want to end my thoughts with a personal touch. It was the year 2019 and I had to be at Tony's recital at Carnegie Hall in New York. As I have mentioned before, he is a tenor, and he was selected to participate in a concert in that wonderful place. It was a moment of great happiness and pride for me as a mother. Never in my life did I imagine that my eldest son would one day be singing in this venue dedicated to the great masters of universal music. Being there was a fantastic recognition to the efforts of our family and especially my Tony!

    We decided to meet that day before the concert, but after his voice rehearsal, since they were preparing all the students. Trying to always be on time, and much more on such an important day, I decided to walk those bustling long streets that reminded me of what I've left behind at JP Morgan Chase to take a much different path many years ago. Immersed in my thoughts on the way to the auditorium, I contemplated how much I've had to walk in my life (literally and emotionally.) Almost without noticing, I sped up, the anticipation for what I was going to enjoy in a few minutes was filling me with tons of energy. In that moment of joy, as in so many other moments of happiness throughout the last years, I imagined how proud *Mami* and *Papi* would've been of their grandson, and then envisioned in my mind all the things they never got to enjoy with us. I walked several more blocks. Deep in my thoughts, I hurried the final steps of that afternoon's journey and as I crossed the street, I asked myself, *How did I get to this moment? How did I do it?* And, as it is my custom, I paused to answer and prayed to God, "Thank you for allowing me to see my children grow up. Thank you for giving me the happiness of knowing that they will turn out to be noble, good, successful, humble, big-hearted men." When I finished crossing, I walked through a well-known park in New York. Unexpectedly, the universe taught me a lesson. All of a sudden, I was standing in front of the statue of Don Benito Juárez García, known as the *Benemérito de las Américas,* who was the president of México long ago and someone who in my childhood and youth I admired so much when reading about his countless contributions as a lawyer. He was the first president of indigenous origin, who with his tenacity and intellect became one of the greatest in the nation. Remembering one of his famous phrases, *"The respect for the rights of others brings peace,"* I was filled with incredible emotion and joy. In that magical instant, all that was left for me was to smile and take the photograph that I share here. It was then that I understood that our heroes and heroines have always existed and that we are the continuation of them. That indigenous blood runs in my veins and it will continue to run in the veins of many future generations. My roots are so deep and long that even in the least expected place they found me and confirmed to me what my mom always said, "It doesn't matter where you come from, but who you choose to be." Therefore, the only way to advance, to progress, to leave a legacy that continues to expand, is to take everyone by the hand and together move forward and continue to rise.

Statue honoring Benito Juárez in Bryant Park, New York. Created by Moisés Cabrera and donated by Oaxaca, México, in 2004.

Former President John F. Kennedy next to Dr. Héctor P. García.

Los Angeles, California, 2019. Giving the highest recognition awarded by the Council for Latino Workplace Equity to Sylvia Méndez (C), of Mexican father and Puerto Rican mother. In 1946, when she was 8, Sylvia testified in court to show that Latinos are as smart as whites. Her case, Méndez v. Westminster, became a precedent in the struggle to desegregate schools in the United States. Thanks to Sylvia and her family, California became the first state to desegregate not only schools, but all public spaces. Her courage paved the way for the landmark Supreme Court case, Brown v. Board of Education, which ended segregation in every school in the nation. Sylvia Méndez was awarded the Presidential Medal of Freedom in 2011.

Winners of the Top National Latino Leaders Award, Los Angeles, California.

Winners of the Top National Latino Leaders Award, Miami, Florida.

While here we keep working for justice… in a hidden street in San Luis Potosí, a darkroom keeps a treasure exactly as my mother left it the last time she visited her studio. Everything is just as she organized it. Bathed in red lights, the trays with chemicals reveal in their quiet seas black and white images; and hanging from the photographer's clothesline, wondrous pictures gently curl under the possessive grip of the pincers. It's Ana's last gift before leaving this world where, for a wonderful but brief moment, she bestowed all of her wisdom on to me.

Thank you Mami for loving and supporting me unconditionally and in such a wise way that you made me believe I could achieve anything I wanted.

We keep moving forward. Everything you gave me with such a generous heart I now share with anyone that wants to follow that same path.

It's my hope that everything you bequeathed me I was able to give to my children. So that they can use that legacy everyday of their lives, no matter what path they take, making sure they always are giving more than they receive.

Life goes on for everyone in the LGBTQ community that has adopted me as an ally. For those who, while following my advice, are also looking for ways to advance equity and justice wherever they go.

My unconditional love also extends to the many individuals I've had the opportunity to spend time with during the many trips, conferences and business meetings held during so many decades.

A great deal of my being is etched unto the walls that listened to my prayers. Truthfully, we are all Her children; we all come from the one who said Yes and offered her own womb so that others may come to be.

You were always the superhero of my life, Ana, my beautiful mother. That's the reason why I shared you with others in these pages, in these recipes, in these nuggets of leadership advice filled with wisdom, your wisdom.

www.ingramcontent.com/pod-product-compliance
Lightning Source LLC
Chambersburg PA
CBHW031641040426
42453CB00006B/171